Praise for

The New Fiduciary Standard

by Tim Hatton, CFP, CIMA, AIF

"Tim Hatton tells fiduciaries exactly what they need to know and does so with clarity and care."

— Burton G. Malkiel
Author, *A Random Walk Down Wall Street*

"Tim Hatton has captured the essential essence of the fundamental requirements of fiduciary responsibility. His practical case-study approach to the application of the 27 Practices identified by the Foundation for Fiduciary Studies, in an easy-to-understand style, is a must-read for anyone having responsibility for 'other people's money.' His explanation of the history and evolution of the current body of knowledge applicable to what has become the 'Fiduciary Standard' is useful for both the novice and experienced professional at every level of advice giving."

— Clark M. Blackman II, CPA/PFS, CFA, CIMA, CFP/AAMS
Partner and Chief Investment Officer, Investec Advisory Group, L.P. (Houston, Texas)

"At last! A book that actually helps fiduciaries apply prudent fiduciary investment standards in a practical way. I strongly recommend that all those who have an interest in modern prudent fiduciary investing—trustees of 401(k) plans, charitable nonprofits, private family trusts, and public employee retirement plans—pick up a copy of Tim Hatton's excellent book, *The New Fiduciary Standard*, and employ its teachings."

— W. Scott Simon, JD, CFP, AIFA
Author, *The Prudent Investor Act: A Guide to Understanding*

"If you could recommend only one book to a financial adviser, it would be Tim Hatton's *The New Fiduciary Standard*. It will change the reader forever. Pandora's box has been opened, never to be closed again."

— Stephen C. Winks
Founder, The Society of Fiduciary Advisors
Founder, Senior Consultant (www.SrConsultant.com)

"For those of us who are beneficiaries or trustees, or who advise them, Tim Hatton's *The New Fiduciary Standard* offers us a way to exercise our fiduciary investment responsibilities, or to advise on them, with excellence. We have long needed such a repository of investment practices to help us make the promises of the Prudent Investor Rule come true. Now we have it with Hatton as our guide!"

— James E. Hughes Jr., Esq.
Author, *Family Wealth—Keeping It in the Family*

AICPA

A Note to the Reader from the AICPA

A RECENT SURVEY conducted by the investment advice firm Financial Engines found that 73 percent of plan sponsors believe their fiduciary responsibilities and liabilities have increased over the past twelve to twenty-four months.[1] And only 48 percent of those plan sponsors surveyed believe they have a clear understanding of their role as a fiduciary.[2] Plan sponsors—particularly small and medium-sized employers—frequently lack the expertise or resources necessary to address the difficult questions posed by fiduciary responsibility.[3]

Investment fiduciaries need help understanding the practical application of their duties. They need materials that will serve as a foundation for prudent investment fiduciary practices and provide investment fiduciaries with an organized process for making informed and consistent decisions.

The AICPA and the Foundation for Fiduciary Studies in 2003 published a definitive guide for investment fiduciaries entitled *Prudent Investment Practices: A Handbook for Investment Fiduciaries* (Handbook). It outlines twenty-seven practices that should be followed by an investment fiduciary to ensure compliance with the various directives provided by ERISA, Department of Labor, SEC, and case law that have evolved in this area over the past thirty years. Every fiduciary today needs to ensure that their responsibilities are being met.

Similarly, this new work, *The New Fiduciary Standard: The 27 Prudent Investment Practices for Financial Advisers, Trustees, and Plan Sponsors,* provides practical application of the Hand-

---

1. Department of Labor Overview of Fiduciary Responsibility Issue; Press Conference on May 18, 2004, Combs, Ann L. (Assistant Secretary of Labor).
2. Id.
3. Id.

book's practices. *The New Fiduciary Standard* helps fiduciaries understand the practical application of their duties, provides a range of reference materials, encourages fiduciaries to adhere to a higher standard, and breeds a high expectation for achievement for both the fiduciary and the client. The text helps the practitioner visualize how to implement the prudent investment practices in a firm of any size.

The New Fiduciary Standard, along with *Prudent Investment Practices,* provides fiduciaries with a knowledge base in the extensive practice area of investment fiduciaries. Fiduciaries must, however, exercise professional judgment when applying the twenty-seven practices; they should consult legal counsel and other authorities when appropriate.

The AICPA supports the establishment and maintenance of the highest fiduciary standards. The processes addressed in *Prudent Investment Practices,* along with the practical applications described in *The New Fiduciary Standard,* will help the current fiduciary better understand his or her role and may provide their clients with better investment performance.

The American Institute of Certified Public Accountants is the ISO 9001-2000 certified national professional organization of CPAs, with approximately 350,000 members, including members serving in business and industry, public practice, government, and education; student affiliates; and international associates. It sets ethical standards for the profession and U.S. private auditing standards. It also develops and grades the Uniform CPA Examination. For more information about the AICPA, please visit ***www.aicpa.org****.*

The New Fiduciary Standard

The New Fiduciary Standard

The 27 Prudent Investment Practices for Financial Advisers, Trustees, and Plan Sponsors

Tim Hatton, CFP, CIMA, AIF

in cooperation with The Foundation for Fiduciary Studies

Legal review for ERISA provisions provided by Fred Reish, Esq., Managing Director at Reish Luftman Reicher & Cohen

BLOOMBERG PRESS

PRINCETON

For data used in the analysis for the table "Inconsistency of Return Premium" on page 57, grateful acknowledgement is made to the Center for Research in Security Prices (CRSP®), Graduate School of Business, The University of Chicago. © 2005 CRSP. Used with permission. All rights reserved. www.crsp.uchicago.org

This publication contains the author's opinions and is designed to provide accurate and authoritative information. It is sold with the understanding that the author, publisher, and Bloomberg L.P. are not engaged in rendering legal, accounting, investment-planning, or other professional advice. The reader should seek the services of a qualified professional for such advice; the author, publisher, and Bloomberg L.P. cannot be held responsible for any loss incurred as a result of specific investments or planning decisions made by the reader.

The investment fiduciary practices contained within *The New Fiduciary Standard* and *Prudent Investment Practices* have not been approved, disapproved, or otherwise acted upon by any senior technical committee of the American Institute of Certified Public Accountants and have no official or authoritative status with respect to the AICPA.

First edition published 2005
1 3 5 7 9 10 8 6 4 2

Library of Congress Cataloging-in-Publication Data

Hatton, Tim
The new fiduciary standard : the 27 prudent investment practices for financial advisers, trustees, and plan sponsors / Tim Hatton, in cooperation with the Foundation for Fiduciary Studies.--1st ed.
p. cm.
"Legal review for ERISA provisions provided by Fred Reish, Esq., managing director at Reish, Luftman, Reicher & Cohen."
Includes bibliographical references and index.
ISBN 1-57660-183-8 (alk. paper)
1. Investment advisors--Legal status, laws, etc.--United States. 2. Financial planners--Legal status, laws, etc.--United States. 3. Trusts and trustees--United States. 4. Investments--Law and legislation--United States. 5. Financial services industry--Law and legislation--United States. I. Foundation for Fiduciary Studies. II. Title.

KF1072.H38 2005
332.6'0973--dc22

2005000707

Acquiring Editor: Jared Kieling
Copy Editor: Edward Mansour

To my parents,
Dr. Richard L. Hatton and Elaine M. Hatton

Contents

FOREWORD

AS OF THIS WRITING, the investment advisory industry—in which I include investment consultants, wealth managers, financial planners, broker consultants, private bankers, and estate planners—is well into its adolescence, but it still lacks the attributes and chiseled profile of a true profession.

➢ There is no oversight by one regulatory body. Some investment advisers are regulated by the National Association of Securities Dealers (NASD), others by the Securities and Exchange Commission (SEC) and/or various state agencies, and still others by the Office of the Comptroller of the Currency.

➢ There are virtually no specific regulations designed for the investment adviser's unique role. Investment advisers are wedged between NASD compliance rules, which are written to address procedures for executing securities transactions and the selling of financial products, and SEC regulations, which are written to provide regulatory oversight for money managers.

➢ There are no defined practice standards covering all investment advisers. There is no standardized "report card" by which the public can determine whether it is receiving the level of care to which it is entitled.

➢ There are no advanced education and training requirements. Barbers and beauticians have more rigorous and more clearly defined educational requirements.

Perhaps the most significant missing attribute of all has been a widely acknowledged, well-articulated *fiduciary standard of care.* Until very recently, there had been little concerted movement within the financial industry in that direction. If anything, some professionals have been at pains to avoid the implications of such a standard, rather than embracing its potential.

The importance of the role of the investment adviser cannot be overstated. More than 5 million men and women serve as investment fiduciaries, with the legal responsibility for managing someone else's money. Moreover, the vast majority of the nation's liquid investable wealth is managed by these same fiduciaries. Investment advisers often are called upon to be the nucleus around which this larger universe of investment fiduciaries forms.

The longstanding need to define the respective roles and responsibilities of fiduciaries and investment advisers has become painfully acute during the recent investment industry scandals. The industry scandals all have one thing in common: a fiduciary parlaying a position of trust into personal profit.

The public is not going to let Wall Street return to business as usual. The public is demanding that Wall Street demonstrate that it is committed to following a higher standard of care, a defined fiduciary standard of care. The public has begun to realize that our nation's wealth is a finite resource, and that we cannot rely on regulations alone for protection. We need to have defined fiduciary practices to aid in distinguishing good investment procedures from bad ones, and good investment advisers from charlatans.

As critical a role as fiduciaries and investment advisers play in ensuring the fiscal health of this nation, the investment industry has never attempted to define the practices these persons should be following in managing investment decisions—until now.

This book, *The New Fiduciary Standard,* is a critical adjunct to the handbook *Prudent Investment Practices,* which was co-produced by the Foundation for Fiduciary Studies and the American Institute of Certified Public Accountants (AICPA) in 2003. That concise handbook was intentionally written to be a general guide, with the anticipation that industry leaders, such as Tim Hatton, would follow up with more specific guidance on how these practices should be implemented.

Sound fiduciary practices often provide the collateral benefit of good investment performance. The fiduciary practices covered in this book have their roots in legislation, case law, and regulatory opinion letters, but they also make good investment sense. Even the assets of nonfiduciary accounts—that is, assets that are not held in any type of trust, whether those be individual and family retail accounts or those of high-net-worth investors—would be better managed by following these fiduciary practices.

It is an honor to be associated with this book and with the efforts Tim Hatton is making to spread the fiduciary message. I encourage all investment fiduciaries and investment advisers to heed his advice. And I urge all investors, trust beneficiaries, and retirement plan participants never to accept a level of fiduciary care that is anything less than what follows.

DONALD B. TRONE

Accredited Investment Fiduciary Auditor® (AIFA)

President, Foundation for Fiduciary Studies

A Summary of the Five Steps and Twenty-Seven Practices

Step One: Analyze Current Position (Practices 1.1–1.6)

PRACTICE 1.1: Investments are managed in accordance with applicable laws, trust documents, and written investment policy statements.

PRACTICE 1.2: Fiduciaries are aware of their duties and responsibilities.

PRACTICE 1.3: Fiduciaries and parties in interest are not involved in self-dealing.

PRACTICE 1.4: Service agreements and contracts are in writing and do not contain provisions that conflict with fiduciary standards of care.

PRACTICE 1.5: There is documentation to show timing and distribution of cash flows and the payment of liabilities.

PRACTICE 1.6: Assets are within the jurisdiction of U.S. courts and are protected from theft and embezzlement.

Step Two: Diversify—Allocate Portfolio (Practices 2.1–2.5)

PRACTICE 2.1: A risk level has been identified.

PRACTICE 2.2: An expected modeled return to meet investment objectives has been identified.

PRACTICE 2.3: An investment time horizon has been identified.

PRACTICE 2.4: Selected asset classes are consistent with the identified risk, return, and time horizon.

PRACTICE 2.5: The number of asset classes is consistent with portfolio size.

Step Three: Formalize Investment Policy (Practices 3.1–3.7)

PRACTICE 3.1: There is detail to implement a specific investment strategy.

PRACTICE 3.2: The investment policy statement defines the duties and responsibilities of all parties involved.

PRACTICE 3.3: The investment policy statement defines diversification and rebalancing guidelines.

PRACTICE 3.4: The investment policy statement defines due diligence criteria for selecting investment options.

PRACTICE 3.5: The investment policy statement defines monitoring criteria for investment options and service vendors.

PRACTICE 3.6: The investment policy statement defines procedures for controlling and accounting for investment expenses.

PRACTICE 3.7: The investment policy statement defines appropriately structured, socially responsible investment strategies (when applicable).

Step Four: Implement Policy (Practices 4.1–4.4)

PRACTICE 4.1: The investment strategy is implemented in compliance with the required level of prudence.

PRACTICE 4.2: The fiduciary is following applicable "safe harbor" provisions (when elected).

PRACTICE 4.3: Investment vehicles are appropriate for the portfolio size.

PRACTICE 4.4: A due-diligence process is followed in selecting service providers, including the custodian.

Step Five: Monitor and Supervise (Practices 5.1–5.5)

PRACTICE 5.1: Periodic reports compare investment performance against an appropriate index, peer group and IPS objectives.

PRACTICE 5.2: Periodic reviews are made of qualitative and/or organizational changes of investment decision makers.

PRACTICE 5.3: Control procedures are in place to periodically review policies for best execution, soft dollars, and proxy voting.

PRACTICE 5.4: Fees for investment management are consistent with agreements and the law.

PRACTICE 5.5: "Finders fees," 12b-1 fees, or other forms of compensation that have been paid for asset placement are appropriately applied, utilized, and documented.

PREFACE

THIS BOOK describes and explains the prudent and disciplined investment process that must be followed by investment fiduciaries who wish to adhere to a uniform *fiduciary* standard of care. Those who should read it include certified public accountants (CPAs), financial consultants of Wall Street firms, financial planners, registered investment advisers, attorneys, trustees of private trusts, retirement plan sponsors, and members of investment committees. Generally speaking, this book is for anyone who has a legal or moral responsibility for managing or making decisions on behalf of someone else's money or property.

In this book I will primarily speak to my colleagues, investment advisers. This group includes financial consultants, financial planners, and registered investment advisers. However, I am equally interested in the other types of fiduciaries (cited above) who might use this book as a reference to ensure that they are aware of their duties and responsibilities. Being aware of those duties and responsibilities is the first step in fulfilling them.

The need for a uniform standard of care is great because of the complexities the financial industry has created in delivering its services. High fees, poor performance, lack of disclosure, and a system devoid of accountability characterize the financial industry. The recent rash of scandals certainly supports this characterization. The primary tenet of fiduciary investing is that the client's interests come first and that their money is managed for their exclusive benefit; the investing public desires and deserves this from the professionals within the financial industry.

The value of investment advice does not lie in investment performance; it lies in a disciplined investment process. What is a disciplined investment process? At minimum it includes clear identification of a client's goals and objectives; identification of a portfolio's specific risk level to meet such goals and objectives; a plan to diversify the portfolio reasonably (i.e., determine asset allocation); a due-diligence process for the objective selection and monitoring of investment options; clear disclosure of all compensation; preparation of reports that show performance after all fees have been deducted; and, most important, preparation of a written investment policy statement that documents the above criteria. It is difficult to see how any client who receives less than this from their adviser is being cared for properly.

Clients who are guided through a disciplined investment process have the best chance of realizing their goals and objectives. Providing this type of investment advice takes commitment and hard work, but it is exceptionally rewarding for both the adviser and the client. The future of investment advice is the fiduciary standard—which is what will truly differentiate the competent advisers from the pack. I believe those advisers adopting the process outlined in this book will be the advisers of choice by the investing public. I ask all those who read this book to please join me in helping raise the level of professionalism in the investment advisory industry, whether you are a legal fiduciary or not, in order to better protect the interests of our clients.

—TIM HATTON

Acknowledgments

THERE ARE MANY at the top of their professions who helped in the writing of this book; thank you all for sharing your valuable time. Special thanks to Bo Cornell, who said "you have a book in you," and for the considerable time he spent reviewing and offering constructive criticism. My knowledge as an investment adviser has taken a quantum leap since my association with Bo began. To all the guys at the Foundation for Fiduciary Studies—the work you do benefits millions of investors. Indirectly, the Foundation is increasingly providing a voice for millions of small investors who otherwise would have none. In particular, I want to thank Rich Lynch; he spent hours reviewing and answering questions for me, exhibiting patience and kindness every step of the way. To my brother, Jim, for his reviews and encouragement; if he had a nickel for every idea I bounced off of him he could stack them to the moon. I am grateful to Scott Simon for editing my writing. He gracefully let me know that I have wonderful ideas but that I should have paid more attention during English class.

Thank you to Dr. Harry Markowitz, a wonderfully kind and personable man, for his review of the chapter on Modern Portfolio Theory. I now wished I worked harder in my calculus class. I want to thank Truman A. Clark, Ph.D., for his review of the Modern Portfolio Theory chapter with specific attention to the Fama-French Three-Factor Model. He possesses complete command of this subject. I also want to thank attorney Fred Reish for his help with ERISA 404(c) fiduciary issues and his comment to "keep it simple, Tim." For his technical review, I thank Clark Blackman. He too has an in-depth knowledge of fiduciary and investment issues and clearly shares the mission to put clients' interests first.

To Jeff Cornell for his help with the charts and illustrations, which help clarify many complicated points within the Fama-French Three-Factor Model. For their encouragement and belief in the mission of Hatton Consulting, Inc., thank you to Shawna and Brian, partners within my firm.

Finally, to my girls, my wife Jen and daughter Heidi: this book is about doing what is right and caring for the interests of others. Thank you for taking such good care of me.

INTRODUCTION

INVESTOR BEHAVIOR is often at odds with sound investment decision making. I have found—and I am sure my adviser colleagues concur—that in my nearly twenty years as an investment adviser the toughest part of my job is managing investor expectations. I created Hatton Consulting, Inc. (transitioning from Morgan Stanley, after twelve years) in April 2000 (perfect timing!). The last two years of the 1990s were somewhat difficult for me. I am sure this was true of other advisers, yet this was contrary to what most advisers were experiencing at the time. This was so because I had to explain time and again why diversification was a sound, long-term investing strategy. Some clients questioned why I had a portion of their money in small-cap value stocks when it was obvious that large-cap growth stocks and initial public offerings (IPOs) were the place to be. One client in particular told me he would not follow me to my new firm because I had lagged the market terribly and would instead move his money to Janus (mind you, this was April 2000). I have not heard from him, but I'm sure his investment outcome is not what he expected. Even though history presents investors with many valuable lessons to investors, history has provided ample evidence that investors, in fact, do not always learn from their mistakes.

This is not a new phenomenon. One of the most famous examples of how irrational investor behavior can lead to investment disaster is the "Tulip Bulb Craze." In 1559, Conrad Gestner introduced tulip bulbs to Holland, and tulips quickly became status symbols for the wealthy. A virus eventually infected the bulbs; but far from killing them, it actually helped set off the "craze" by creating a more colorful and desirable tulip. As a result, the popularity of tulips spread beyond the wealthy to the common folk of Dutch society. As prices rose higher, bulbs began to be formally traded on organized local market exchanges.

By 1634, people of the middle class saw friends and family profit wildly and thought this trend would continue into the unforeseeable future. At the height of the craze in 1635, the value of a single rare tulip bulb was equivalent to four tons of wheat, eight tons of rye, one bed, four oxen, eight pigs, twelve sheep, one suit of clothes, two casks of wine, four tons of beer, two tons of butter, one thousand pounds of cheese, and one silver cup! The estimated present-day value of all these items is $35,000.[1] In 1636, the belief that the prices of tulip bulbs would continue to rise forever suddenly disappeared, and some people began to sell. When widespread panic set in among the tulip bulb owners the government ordered all contracts between sellers and buyers to be settled at 10 percent of the original contract price. This decree, as well as others, however, failed to stabilize the tulip bulb market, so that by 1637 bulbs that were once valued at $35,000 worth of goods now sold for less than $1.[2]

The Problem

The meltdown in the stock market from 2000 to 2002 is just the latest example of how the age-old problem of irrational human behavior can result in a modern-day "tulip mania." Many investors bought tens of thousands of dollars' worth of stocks that had no records of earnings, much less any profits. What happened in this stock market run-up and subsequent decline was not much different, at its emotional core, than the tulip craze.

The stock market's spectacular rise in the 1980s and 1990s had many investors believing that it was their "right" to earn portfolio returns of 20 percent or even 40 percent, or more. They came to see the stock market as a giant casino where they couldn't seem to lose. The occasional short-term dips that occurred during this rise were seen by many as "buying opportunities" that presented investors with more chances to amass additional wealth.

More and more investors came to believe that Warren Buffet's method of investing—buying the stocks of companies that actually produced profits—was a sucker's bet. The laws of investing seemed to be thrown out the window; an investment revolution appeared to be taking place as "New Economy" stocks continued their improbable rise in value. Fueling this speculative behavior were stories appearing in the media describing how secretaries at companies such as Amazon.com and Yahoo were becoming millionaires seemingly overnight. (This underscores the complicity of the media in helping to promote the stock market "bubble" by highlighting and sensationalizing the rare instances of huge investor gains.) Twenty-something college dropouts were becoming millionaires or even billionaires (at least on paper) as their start-up companies went public soon after their founding. Human nature being what it is, everyone wanted a piece of the action.

Meanwhile, rogue executives at some well-known and long-established publicly traded companies "cooked" the books to fraudulently increase earnings at their companies. For example, WorldCom was secretly fabricating more than $4 billion in company revenues, and Enron was in the process of building an investment house of cards. This drove up the prices of each company's stock, which made it all the more profitable for these executives to cash in their stock options. These actions helped to bid up stock prices of other companies as well, moving the market averages higher and higher. A classic case of good old-fashioned greed was taking place, evidenced by both the unethical and illegal conduct of corporate insiders *and* the investing public.

By the end of 2002, the broad stock market (represented by the S&P 500 index) had declined by about 45 percent in value. The technology-heavy Nasdaq experienced a crash similar to that in 1929, falling approximately 80 percent in value from its peak value in early 2000. Many investors grew frightened over the shrinking values of their investment portfolios and began to question the value of investing in financial markets, particularly the stock market. Confidence had been shaken by the corporate scandals of WorldCom and Enron and the fraudulent research prepared by Wall Street brokerage firms. Investor confidence was again shaken in September 2003 when New York Attorney General Elliot Spitzer began to expose the hidden and illegal arrangements at many mutual fund families in a complaint filed in New York state court. Spitzer charged a number of fund companies with market timing (which usually is not illegal) and late trading (which always is illegal). These companies allowed a select few to "late-trade" their funds, allowing certain traders to make decisions after the current day's closing price was known. The "squeaky-clean" image of America's vast mutual fund industry was sullied by the business practices of many in the industry that were exposed.

Why do investment manias occur? The answers can be complex, but it seems they occur mainly because investors pile into the markets to "chase performance" in response to sharply increasing market values and the easy profits they engender.

When the run-up in value stretches over a long period of time, such as during 1995 to 1999, when large company growth stocks experienced spectacular returns and investors were rewarded for chasing performance, the next typical mistake of investor behavior occurs: overconfidence. At this point investors start to believe that the superior returns they are experiencing are a result of their investment skill, when in fact it is primarily luck. Once overconfidence sets in, speculative behavior replaces prudent investment behavior as investors focus more and more on increasingly flawed (yet attractive) investment ideas at the expense of investing intelligently in a portfolio as a whole. As a result, investor behavior becomes completely disconnected from sound investment principles.

The Evidence

Many investors and advisers believe they suffered during the market meltdown of 2000–2002 because of the dishonest actions of a few. It's my own belief, however, that the amount of money lost in the financial markets through outright fraud is dwarfed by the amount that has been lost by *misguided investment practices.* As Benjamin Graham, legendary mentor to Warren Buffet and author of *The Intelligent Investor,* said: "The investor's chief problem—and even his worst enemy—is likely to be himself."

Many investors (both amateur *and professional*) routinely make investment decisions without an accurate understanding of how financial markets work. This was particularly true in the late 1990s and into 2000 when these investors completely lost sight of the fundamental difference between *investing* and *speculating.* In fact, many investors simply do not understand the damaging effects that market timing, poor stock picking, poor diversification, high costs and taxes, and other such variables can have on the value of their investment portfolios. There is no doubt that the government must guarantee that financial markets provide an honest and level playing field for all investors—but investors also need to take personal responsibility for their own investment decisions and actions and ensure that they are based on sound investment principles.

Strong evidence showing how investors lose money as a result of their own (or their advisers') poor investment decision making is found in a highly regarded study conducted by DALBAR Financial Services.[3] Among the study's findings for the period 1984–2002 is that the average stock investor underperformed the S&P 500 index of stocks by almost 10 percentage points per year. In addition, a *Forbes* magazine article[4] estimated in 2003 that poor investment decisions made by investors in the 1990s resulted in total losses of $1 trillion! The DALBAR study concluded: "Investment return is far more dependent on investment behavior than on fund performance. Mutual fund investors who simply remained invested earned higher real investor returns than those who attempted to time the market."

The Solution: Managing Investor Behavior

A significant concern for advisers and other fiduciaries that put the interests of their clients first is to ensure that the behavior of clients is in full alignment with sound investment principles. A careful reading of this book should allow you to establish and implement the sound and well-defined investment process that it describes. That process can form the basis of a world-class investment experience for your clients by compelling them to adhere to sound investment decision making. At every twist of the journey through up markets and down markets, times of war and peace, economic upturns and downturns, and life-changing events, managing a well-defined investment process is the answer to managing investor behavior.

Credibility of the Solution: Foundation for Fiduciary Studies

The handbook, *Prudent Investment Practices: A Handbook for Investment Fiduciaries,* written by the Foundation for Fiduciary Studies (Foundation), forms the basis on which this book was written. (For guidance on how to obtain a copy of *Prudent Investment Practices,* please see the final page of this book.) The Foundation for Fiduciary Studies is a not-for-profit, standards-setting organization that has as its mission to develop and promote the Practices that define a prudent process for investment fiduciaries. There are Twenty-Seven *Practices* outlined by the Foundation that make up its prudent investment process. There are two companies associated with the Foundation: the Center for Fiduciary Studies (CFS) is the training entity that operates in association with the Center for Executive Education at the University of Pittsburgh Joseph M. Katz Graduate School of Business. It is at the CFS where you can study and earn the Accredited Investment Fiduciary™ and the Accredited Investment Fiduciary Auditor™ certifications. Fiduciary Analytics is the technology arm that develops web-based tools based on the fiduciary practices for investment decision makers.

I set out to write this book because I found that as a result of speaking with CPAs, attorneys, and other advisers or fiduciaries, there was no comprehensive source that could tell them how to implement the Twenty-Seven Practice Standards described in the Foundation's handbook.

My book carefully describes the investment process that I use at my own investment advisory firm. That process is modeled on the Twenty-Seven Practice Standards established by the Foundation. The model that I use includes much of the technology and tools developed by the Foundation to make implementation of the process easier. You will see that I have added more direction to some of the Practices, while some can be easily implemented with little further explanation from me. The Foundation has given me permission to write about its Practices and quote them verbatim from the Foundation's handbook to ensure consistency. Since incorporating the Practices into my investment advisory practice, I have found that nearly any question asked by an investor can be answered in a concise and clear manner by reference to the Foundation's Practices.

The term *fiduciary* is defined by the Foundation to include those that (1) have a legal or moral responsibility for managing property for the benefit of another; (2) exercise discretion, authority, or control over assets; and (3) act in a professional capacity of trust and render investment advice. The more than five million fiduciaries in America include investment advisers that manage someone else's money on a comprehensive and continuous basis; investment committee members and named trustees, even when they have delegated investment responsibility to agents; and professionals such as accountants, attorneys, actuaries, and consultants when they materially participate in investment decisions.

The Foundation has developed a five-step investment management process, as shown in the table below.

Each of the five steps of the process has a number of Practices associated with it. These twenty-seven Practices are the "meat" hanging on the "bones" of the five steps comprising this investment process.

Five-Step Investment Management Process

Step One	Analyze Current Position
Step Two	Diversify–Allocate Portfolio
Step Three	Formalize Investment Policy
Step Four	Implement Policy
Step Five	Monitor and Supervise

Source: Foundation for Fiduciary Studies

Step One: Analyze Current Position

Practices 1.1–1.6 comprise Step One. The primary objective of this step is to fully understand the current position of the client or trust. This includes identifying their assets and liabilities, current asset allocation, goals and objectives, philanthropic and estate planning desires, tax status, knowledge level of the financial markets, past investing experiences, and emotional tolerance for risk. Identifying the duties and responsibilities of all parties involved (including the client) in the management of the portfolio should also be outlined.

Step Two: Diversify—Allocate Portfolio

Practices 2.1–2.5 comprise Step Two. The primary objective of this step is to determine the risk tolerance of the portfolio/client, the modeled return needed to realize the stated goals and objectives of the client or trust, and the specific sub-asset classes that will be used to construct the portfolio.

Step Three: Formalize Investment Policy

Practices 3.1–3.7 comprise Step Three. The primary objective of this step is to prepare a *written* investment policy statement (IPS). The IPS is a document that serves as the business plan and the communication device for directing the activities of the investment program. Some of the most important components of the IPS include the duties and responsibilities of all parties involved in the management of the portfolio, diversification and rebalancing guidelines, the due-diligence process for selecting and monitoring investment options and service vendors, as well as the policy for accounting for investment expenses.

Step Four: Implement Policy

Practices 4.1–4.4 comprise Step Four. Advisers/fiduciaries must determine what aspects of the investment plan they can personally implement and what needs to be delegated to professionals. Applying the due-diligence process outlined in the IPS will aid in the identification of specific money managers and others responsible for managing the assets of the portfolio.

Step Five: Monitor and Supervise

Practices 5.1–5.5 comprise Step Five, the final step. Periodic reviews, at least quarterly, are conducted to ensure that appropriate progress is being made. Reports should be maintained to determine quarter-to-date, year-to-date, and inception-to-date performance so that the entire portfolio can be compared against appropriate benchmark portfolios. Individual investment options also should be compared against appropriate indices to determine whether the investment objectives are being met. Service providers are also evaluated to ensure they are performing in accordance with written agreements, including an evaluation of all fees pertaining to the management of portfolio assets.

Historical Background

The Practices are rooted in early trust law dating back to as early as eleventh-century England. The following constitutes a sort of "historical horseback ride" through the development of trust investment law in America.

Prudent Man Rule (1830) The standard of trust investment law in America was established in the 1830 Massachusetts case of *Harvard College v. Amory*. Immediately prior to this case,

English common law dictated that the only suitable investments for trusts were government bonds and bank securities. But in early nineteenth-century America, there were few government bonds and bank securities that were considered as safe as British ones. Instead, many trustees had to invest in the stocks of American "start-up" companies of the day. That is ultimately why the Massachusetts court eased the inflexible English standard of investing solely in government and bank securities.

The *Harvard College* case created what became known as the "Prudent Man Rule": trustees should "observe how men of prudence, discretion and intelligence manage their own affairs, not in regard to speculation, but in regard to the permanent disposition of their funds, considering the probable income, as well as the probable safety of the capital to be invested." The Prudent Man Rule created a broad and flexible standard that trustees could follow when investing and courts could use when that investment conduct was challenged legally.

Legal List Rule (mid-1800s) By the middle of the nineteenth century, courts began transforming the broad and flexible *Harvard College* principles into narrow rules in which many assets were deemed "speculative" per se. For example, investing in second mortgages was considered imprudent as a matter of law. The "Legal List Rule," which mandated a narrow set of investments suitable for trusts such as long-term government and corporate bonds, replaced the Prudent Man rule in many states.

Prudent Man Rule Statute (1942) As America entered the twentieth century and became more industrialized, financial markets became more sophisticated. In 1942, the American Bankers Association adopted the Prudent Man Rule Statute. This model law closely followed the Prudent Man Rule set forth in *Harvard College*. Prudent Man Rule Statute allowed trustees to invest in more than government and corporate bonds. Many of them, however, remained reluctant to venture outside of "safe" investments for fear of liability from losses.

Uniform Management of Institutional Funds Act (1972) The Ford Foundation conducted a series of studies in the 1960s that found the portfolios at many leading educational institutions to be invested too conservatively, which resulted in generation of insufficient returns. The issuance of the Uniform Management of Institutional Funds Act in 1972 was a response to these studies. The primary goal of this model law was to allow educational, charitable, religious, and government institutions to adopt a policy of "total return investing" for their investment portfolios.

Employee Retirement Income Security Act (1974) The Employee Retirement Income Security Act (ERISA) was enacted by Congress in 1974. This comprehensive federal pension law was a response to the abuses of some that were responsible for retirement plans in the 1950s and 1960s. These plans included the Teamsters' Western States Pension Fund, which was outright looted by union officials, and the Studebaker Automobile Company Pension Plan, which was not adequately funded by the company. In both examples, the participants in the plans failed to receive their promised retirement benefits. ERISA was intended to ensure that such benefits were actually paid to employees.

ERISA is strict in its requirement that the fiduciaries of a qualified retirement plan, such as a 401(k) plan, discharge their duties *solely* in the interests of participants and their beneficiaries:

- For the exclusive purpose of providing benefits to plan participants and beneficiaries and defraying reasonable expenses of plan administration;
- With the care, prudence, and diligence under the circumstances then prevailing that a prudent man acting in a like

capacity and familiar with such matters would use in the conduct of and enterprise of a like character and with like aims;

➢ By diversifying the investments of the plan so as to minimize the risk of large losses, unless under the circumstances it is clearly prudent not to do so; and

➢ In accordance with plan documents insofar as they are consistent with ERISA.

ERISA fiduciaries are *personally liable* for any investment losses suffered by participants in qualified retirement plans that the fiduciaries cause because of their imprudent conduct.

Restatement 3rd of Trusts (Prudent Investor Rule) (1992) The Restatement 3rd of Trusts (Prudent Investor Rule) ("Restatement") was issued in 1992. This landmark reformation of law restates the basic rules governing the investment of trust assets. The introduction to the Restatement notes: "This Restatement is a guide for practitioners of law, trustees and investment advisers as well as a source of legal authority."

One of the primary reasons for drafting the Restatement was to incorporate concepts of Modern Portfolio Theory. This theory (discussed in detail in Part One) is a body of academic writings whose principles were first set forth more than fifty years ago. Modern Portfolio Theory, though, is much more than a compilation of academic writing and scholarly thought. In fact, its principles have been put to wide use in the real world of investing where they govern the investment of hundreds of billions of dollars. The originators of Modern Portfolio Theory were awarded for their efforts with the 1990 Nobel Prize in Economic Sciences.

It is important to note that Modern Portfolio Theory is not known as Modern *Investment* Theory for good reason: The most important unit in investing is *the portfolio as a whole,* not individual parts of it. There is a tendency by professional money managers who have done a poor job at the portfolio level to shift the focus away from the performance to a component of the portfolio that has performed well. In fact, as I discuss in more detail in Practice 4.1, the Restatement is clear that passive as well as active investment strategies are prudent. However, there is a greater burden of proof for those utilizing active strategies to show that their efforts are in fact adding value. Prudent fiduciaries, however, must remain focused on the entire trust portfolio and the investment strategy on which it is based.

The Introduction to the Restatement defines five principles of prudence that must be followed by fiduciaries subject to the rules of the Restatement:

1) Sound diversification is fundamental to risk management and is therefore ordinarily required of trustees.

2) Risk and return are so directly related that trustees have a duty to analyze and make conscious decisions concerning the levels of risk appropriate to the purposes, distribution requirements, and other circumstances of the trusts they administer.

3) Trustees have a duty to avoid fees, transactions costs, and other expenses that are not justified by needs and realistic objectives of the trust's investment program.

4) The fiduciary duty of impartiality requires a balancing of the elements of return between production of current income and the protection of purchasing power.

5) Trustees may have a duty as well as having the authority to delegate as prudent investors would.

Uniform Prudent Investor Act (1994) The Uniform Prudent Investor Act (UPIA) is a codification of the Restatement and incorporates many of its principles. The prefatory note to the UPIA notes: "The Uniform Prudent Investor Act undertakes to update trust investment law in recognition of the alterations that have occurred in investment practice. These changes have occurred under the influence of a large and broadly accepted body of empirical and theoretical knowledge about the behavior of capital markets, often described as 'modern portfolio theory.'"

The prefatory note to the UPIA also notes that the UPIA primarily regulates the activities of trustees of private family trusts. It also is made clear in other parts of the UPIA that the UPIA also bears on the investment conduct of fiduciaries responsible for the assets of ERISA pension plans and public employee retirement plans, as well as charitable nonprofits.

The prefatory note to the UPIA identifies five fundamental alterations in the former criteria for prudent investing (all are also found in the Restatement):

1) The standard of prudence is applied to any investment as part of the total portfolio (all assets) rather than to that investment individually.

2) The trade-off in all investing between risk and return is identified as the fiduciary's central consideration.

3) All categorical restrictions on types of investments have been abrogated; the trustee can invest in anything that plays an appropriate role in achieving the risk/return objectives of the trust and that meets the other requirements of prudent investing.

4) The definition of prudent investing integrates the requirement that fiduciaries diversify their investments.

5) Delegation of trust investment and management functions is now permitted, subject to safeguards.

Uniform Management of Public Employee Retirement Systems Act (1997) The summary to the Uniform Management of Public Employee Retirement Systems Act (UMPERSA) describes what it means for fiduciaries to hold assets *in trust:* "By declaring that all retirement system assets are held in trust, [UMPERSA] assures that public employees are guaranteed the highest standard of conduct in the management and investment of assets for retirement that the law can establish. A trustee is the highest fiduciary, carries the greatest burdens of care, loyalty, and utmost good faith for the beneficiaries to whom he or she is responsible."

The table at right, "Legislation and Oversight Bodies of Investor Groups," identifies six different groups of investors, and the legislation that governs their investment activities, as well as the oversight bodies that enforce such provisions. Although the five-step process in this book provides the foundation for an investment process for each type of investor, I faced a significant challenge in writing this book due to the fact that each group possesses unique circumstances and characteristics. For example, individual and family accounts that are not governed by a trust do not have any direct legislation or oversight body monitoring them; how this group implements the Practices will differ from retirement accounts governed by ERISA. In addition, all twenty-seven Practices may not pertain to every group. Therefore, I ask the reader to understand this fact by carefully considering the unique needs and circumstances of whatever group you may be consulting with and how each Practice may or may not apply.

The five-step process and the Practices associated with each step that have been developed by the Foundation for Fiduciary Studies are derived from the foregoing model acts and ERISA. It is incumbent on all professional investment advisers that serves as fiduciaries to gain a good understanding of the twenty-seven Practices that are described and explained in this book. Investment professionals cannot take their fiduciary responsibilities lightly. Indeed, failure to know these fiduciary duties is no legal defense; as one court put it: "A pure heart and empty head is no defense." The better practice for nonfiduciary investment advisers would be to follow the five-step process as well.

Any investment adviser—fiduciary or nonfiduciary—that implements the process described in these Practices should feel

Legislation and Oversight Bodies of Investor Groups

INVESTOR GROUPS	LEGISLATION	OVERSIGHT BODY
Corporate Retirement Plans	ERISA	DOL, IRS, and PBGC
Public Retirement Plans	UMPERSA	State Attorney General
Taft-Hartley Plans	ERISA	PBGC, DOL, and IRS
Foundations/Endowments	UPIA	State Attorney General
Private Trusts	UPIA	State Courts
Individual and Family[5]		

Note: DOL: Department of Labor; IRS: Internal Revenue Service; PBGC: Pension Benefit Guaranty Corporation; ERISA: Employee Retirement Income Security Act; UPIA: Uniform Prudent Investor Act; UMPERSA: Uniform Management of Public Employee Retirement Systems Act.

Source: Foundation for Fiduciary Studies

confident that they are living up to the responsibilities they owe their clients. It is, after all, process that determines prudent fiduciary conduct, not portfolio performance, according to principles of modern prudent investing. And although prudent conduct is not determined by investment performance, one of the most powerful reasons to implement the twenty-seven Practices of the Foundation's five-step process is that in many cases investment performance can improve significantly as a result.

PART ONE

Modern Portfolio Theory

Chapter One

Early Years

ERISA, the Restatement, the UPIA, and other sources of law that govern the activities of fiduciaries have clearly accepted and adopted many findings of Modern Portfolio Theory. Understanding the following concepts should lead to more informed investment decisions as well as provide sound rationale if those decisions are ever questioned. I am confident the following historical discussion will provide the depth of knowledge needed by fiduciaries. It is presented not to favor passive or active investment strategies, because both are prudent when carried out in a disciplined manner; rather, it is presented in order to provide the knowledge necessary to effectively evaluate either strategy.

On October 16, 1990, the Alfred Nobel Memorial Prize in Economic Sciences was awarded to Harry M. Markowitz of the City University of New York, William F. Sharpe of Stanford University, and Merton H. Miller of the University of Chicago for their pioneering work in the field of financial economics. Markowitz had single-handedly established this branch of economics in 1952 upon publication of a fourteen-page paper titled "Portfolio Selection." This paper was the seminal work for what became known as Modern Portfolio Theory. This theory comprises a broad academic body of research that seeks to explain the relationship between investment risk and return. Markowitz's fellow Nobel laureate Merton Miller later characterized this paper as the "big bang" of all modern finance. As a result, Markowitz is universally acknowledged as the father of Modern Portfolio Theory.

The awarding of Nobel prizes to Markowitz, Sharpe, and Miller was a milestone because it formally recognized the revolution in investment theory and practice that began nearly forty years earlier upon publication of Markowitz's paper. Any revolution, by definition, must be a radical change *from* the state of affairs that preceded it. In order to appreciate the contributions of these Nobel laureates, then, it's necessary to review the state of affairs that existed in the investment world previous to the revolution they launched.

Pre Markowitz

Prior to the 1950s, when Markowitz first set forth his theory, the investment world was far different. Stockbrokers focused on selecting relatively few stocks and bonds for their clients. This approach was typified by Gerald M. Loeb, a leading stockbroker on Wall Street in the 1930s. In his 1935 best-seller, *The Battle for Investment Survival*, he observed: "Once you attain competency, diversification is undesirable. One or two, or at most, three or four securities should be bought. Competent investors will never be satisfied beating the market averages by a few small percentage points." Within the investment community, it was widely believed that careful study of individual securities would enable an investor to identify undervalued companies, which would lead to market-beating performance. Concentrating on finding a few securities with the highest expected return, then, was the investment strategy of the day. There was little or no assessment of risk or concern for diversification.

It was widely assumed in those days—as it is today—that "professional" investors regularly outperformed the market. One prominent individual, however, questioned this assumption in 1931. Alfred Cowles III was president of the investment firm Cowles and Company. His firm was one of many that published forecasting advice on the stock market. Cowles came to believe that the advice his investment firm (as well as others) dispensed to clients was not providing them with what he implicitly promised: the ability to predict the stock market. In a startling admission for its day (or any day for that matter), Cowles decided to discontinue his advisory service to his clients because he believed that his forecasting was nothing more than a lot of guesswork.

But Cowles was not ready to retire—far from it. He decided to study the value of advice provided by investment services in a more formalized way. Cowles enlisted the aid of some of the brightest minds in the fields of mathematics, finance, and economics. This collaboration resulted in the formation of the Cowles Commission for Research in Economics in 1932. The first project of the Cowles Commission was to construct stock indices in order to create a benchmark against which investment services could be measured.

Upon completing construction of the indices in 1933, the commission published one of its most noteworthy contributions to investment research: *Can Stock Market Forecasters Forecast?* The short answer to the question posed by the title of this study: "It is doubtful."[1] The Cowles Commission study concluded that investors achieved better investment returns when they could invest in the stock market as a whole rather than pick certain stocks in which to invest.

This conclusion was supported by three separate findings of the Commission. First, the commission recorded the weekly stock purchase recommendations made by sixteen noteworthy investment services for the period of 1928–1932. The Commission found that had an investor invested equal amounts in each recommended purchase over that period of time, he would have underperformed the stock market as a whole by about 1½ percent per year. Second, the commission compared the track record of twenty large fire insurance companies for the same period and found that their performances lagged the stock market as a whole by about 1 percent per year. Third, for the same period the commission recorded the forecasted level of the stock market by twenty-four financial publications. The Commission found that had an investor followed the forecasts by investing equally in each, she would have underperformed the stock market as a whole by about 4 percent per year.

Professional investment advisory firms naturally criticized the study. Indeed, Cowles himself said many years later: "Of course I got a lot of complaints. Who appointed me to keep track? Also, I had belittled the profession of investment adviser. I used to tell them it isn't a profession, and of course that got them even madder. Market advice for a fee is a paradox. Anybody who really knew just wouldn't share his knowledge. Why should he? In five years, he could be the richest man in the world. Why pass the word on?"[2]

The Cowles Commission study was the first time that the expertise of professional money managers and the value of their advice had ever been challenged in a systematic way. The claims made by the status quo of the investment industry had never before been subjected to critical examination. The commission's study found those claims to be woefully lacking.

The importance of this and other findings made by the Cowles Commission cannot be overstated.[3] The commission (still in existence nearly seventy-five years later, now at Yale University) planted the first seeds of doubt about the claims that professional money managers made about their ability to provide investors with market-beating performance. It was not until nearly twenty years later, though, that those seeds reached full germination in the mind of a twenty-three-year-old graduate student in economics at the University of Chicago. The student's name was Harry Markowitz, and the theory that he formed was nothing less than an investment revolution.

Harry Markowitz and "Portfolio Selection" (1952)

Harry Markowitz began the forty-year journey to his Nobel prize by publishing his seminal paper on Modern Portfolio Theory while working at the Cowles Commission on the campus at the University of Chicago. John H. Langbein, the reporter for the Uniform Prudent Investor Act and the Chancellor Kent Professor of Law and Legal History at Yale University Law School, has this to say about Modern Portfolio Theory: "A Copernican revolution...the most fundamental thing that has happened to the investment process—the development of Modern Portfolio Theory, the Theory of Efficient Markets, the scientific understanding of risk/return relationships and the importance of diversification in portfolios."

So what was so revolutionary about Markowitz and his theory? As noted, prior to the publication of his theory professional money managers advised investors to identify a few stocks with the highest expected return and invest in them. In short, they were concerned with attempting to maximize investment return. They showed little or no concern for risk or diversification. Indeed, in Gerald Loeb's best-selling book he had stated unequivocally that diversification of risk is "undesirable."

Markowitz knew, however, that *investors aren't interested just in return—they're concerned with risk as well.* For example, while an investor might want to hold one stock in his portfolio that will surge in value, he knows intuitively that it's very unlikely that will ever happen. The risk that one stock will go down in value—and maybe even stay there for a long time—is precisely why most investors don't invest all their money in one stock. Markowitz knew that investors do indeed pay attention to risk, that risk is central to the whole process of investing.

What made Markowitz such a revolutionary is that he was able to demonstrate mathematically how *stocks that are individually risky lose much of their risk when properly combined together in a portfolio.*[4] In devising his theory, Markowitz drew a distinction between the riskiness of an individual stock and the riskiness of a portfolio (i.e., a collection of stocks and/or bonds).[5] What's noteworthy about this discovery is that it allows investors to not only reduce the riskiness of their portfolios but also (in certain cases) increase investment returns.

Markowitz set out to devise a way to help investors apply rational tradeoffs between risk and return. His efforts resulted in what became known as an "efficient portfolio." A portfolio is said to be *efficient* when it offers an investor the highest expected return for a given level of risk, or the lowest level of risk for a given expected return. Markowitz knew, however, that investors have different preferences for risk and return; some prefer more return and others prefer less risk.

His solution was to set forth what became known as the "efficient frontier," which is comprised solely of efficient portfolios. An investor can select from any one of those portfolios that comports with the investor's unique risk/return profile. The graph at right, "The Efficient Frontier," shows two efficient portfolios located at points A and B that lie on the efficient frontier. A portfolio is said to be *inefficient* when it fails to offer an investor the highest expected return for a given level of risk, or the lowest level of risk for a given expected return. Point C in the graph is an example of an inefficient portfolio, so it does not lie on the efficient frontier.

The Efficient Frontier

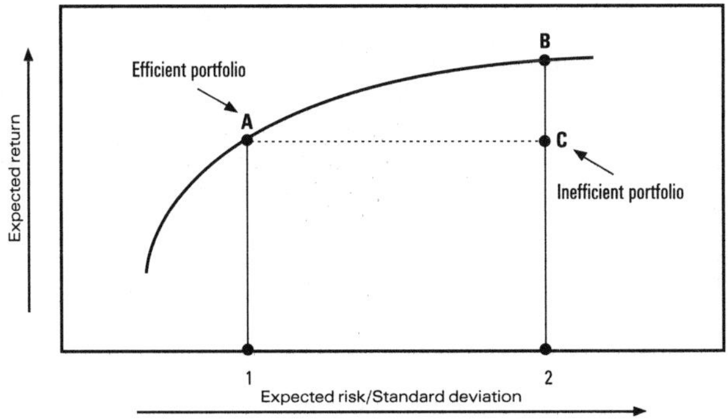

Source: Hatton Consulting, Inc.

The way in which Markowitz actually constructed portfolios was done with a mathematical concept known as "mean variance optimization." A portfolio built through this process from a basket of risky assets is one that is efficient: that is, it maximizes expected return for a given level of risk or minimizes risk for a given level of expected return.

The process of mean variance optimization requires determining the values of three portfolio variables. The first variable is the expected return of each security that is being considered for inclusion in the portfolio; expected returns are determined through a combination of using historical data and/or judgments by securities analysts. The second variable is the expected standard deviation of each such security. The third variable required is the expected correlation between each security in the portfolio. It was, however, Markowitz's use of standard deviation as a measure of risk and the notion of correlation that had never before been used to construct portfolios.

Markowitz used standard deviation to measure the volatility of a security or an asset class of securities. These two terms—

Portfolio Theory's Measure of Risk: Standard Deviation

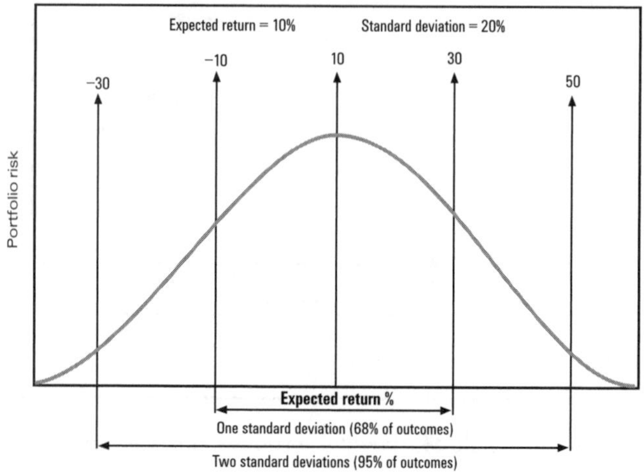

Source: Center for Fiduciary Studies

standard deviation and volatility—are just shorthand for risk. What is risk? Risk is present when there are many more possible outcomes than the particular outcome that is expected. Standard deviation is a mathematical expression that measures the range of possible outcomes. The greater the range of possible outcomes, the higher the standard deviation (or risk or uncertainty) of that security or asset class of securities. For example, the graph above, "Portfolio Theory's Measure of Risk: Standard Deviation," depicts the approximate return and risk (i.e., standard deviation) of the S&P 500 index for the period 1926–2003. The S&P 500 averaged approximately 10% return per year during that period of time while its standard deviation has averaged about 20% annually. That 20% standard deviation was computed by including all the annual returns of the S&P 500 index from 1926 to 2003.

Those annual returns included a high of +53.9% in 1933 and a low of –43.3% in 1931. In order for an investor to achieve a long-term average return of 10%, then, they had to endure a range of possible outcomes that fell somewhere between a +53.9% and a –43.3%, a range of nearly 100 percentage points! Standard deviation illustrates the riskiness inherent in an asset class of securities; other asset classes exhibit even greater ranges of returns.

Markowitz used something else that had never been used before to construct portfolios: the notion of *correlation,* which measures to what degree, positively or negatively, the movements of two variables are associated. In the financial world, correlation is used to identify securities whose returns do not move in lock-step with one another. All risky securities have times when they rise or fall in value; the idea is to add securities to a portfolio that rise and fall in dissimilar ways at dissimilar times. Adding the right securities to a portfolio that is correlated in the right manner has the effect of canceling out much of the *portfolio's* risk. For example, in an inflationary environment where interest rates are rising, utility stocks tend to fall in value. Oil stocks, however, tend to rise in value because inflation forces the price of oil to go up; in turn, oil profits are driven higher. In this scenario, a portfolio containing one utility stock and one oil stock will tend to be less volatile (i.e., a lower standard deviation or less risk) than a portfolio of two utility stocks or a portfolio of two oil stocks. Note that Markowitz was not concerned with the risk of each security in a portfolio but with the effect each security had on the risk of the *whole portfolio.*

The practical application of Markowitz's theories was extremely restricted due to the limitations of computing power in the 1950s. Computing power was obviously much less than what it is today, and the mathematics involved in determining the values of the three variables—expected return, standard deviation, and correlation—required for mean variance optimization was very cumbersome. For example, to run an optimization for a portfolio of only 50 securities required as many as 1,225 calculations; by the time the entire universe of 2,000 stocks (in existence at that time) was analyzed, more than two million calculations were necessary! William Sharpe, who worked under Markowitz, reported it took 33 minutes to solve an optimization for a portfolio of 100 securities.[6] Today, it takes a fraction of a second.

So even though Markowitz's theory was innovative, its practical application was virtually impossible. Modern computers fortunately have solved this problem, and investment advisers are now able to run optimizations at lightning speeds from their desktop computers. Markowitz's pioneering work has led to a tool called portfolio optimization software. Even though this software can be very helpful to investors, it does have its shortcomings. I will discuss in Practices 2.1 through 2.5 how I employ this tool to help identify a risk level for an investor and what I believe are some of its do's and don'ts.

There were a number of other developments in financial theory and practice between the advent of Modern Portfolio in the early 1950s and Markowitz's receipt of his Nobel prize in 1990.

Center for Research in Security Prices (CRSP) (1964)

An article written by James Lorie and Lawrence Fisher, two professors at the University of Chicago's Graduate School of Business, appeared in the January 1964 issue of the university's prestigious *Journal of Business.* The article set forth the first comprehensive measurement of the performance of all common stocks listed on the New York Stock Exchange from 1926 through 1960. The two professors had obtained and compiled their data from the Center for Research in Security Prices (CRSP) located at the University of Chicago. In 1960, Merrill Lynch had granted $300,000 to the University of Chicago to fund a project to essentially answer the question: "How much return do stock investors actually earn?" Up to that point, amazingly, no one knew!

Lorie and Fisher accumulated a staggering amount of statistical calculations estimated at between two million and three million pieces of data. Both academic researchers and investment professionals were astonished at their findings. For example, an investor who invested $1,000 in the stock market in 1926, reinvested all dividends, paid no taxes, and remained fully invested until the end of 1960 would have accumulated nearly $30,000, or a gain of about 9 percent a year. In light of the fact that many investors in 1964 still had vivid memories of the Great Depression and its stock market crash, 9 percent a year was much more than most of them would have thought. This investment return was far greater than what an investor would have earned from bonds or savings bank deposits during those years. For the first time, investors had some comprehensive historical investment data at hand that gave them a sense of how common stocks performed vis-à-vis other investments. The data also allowed investors to compare and analyze their own investment results.

Another landmark study also relied on data obtained from the CRSP database. Roger G. Ibbotson and Rex A. Sinquefield, two recent graduates of the Graduate School of Business at the University of Chicago, authored the study, published in 1976. The study was the first to compile and present in an organized way historical investment data on stocks and bonds;[7] they also reported data on inflation.

The Ibbotson-Sinquefield data, now updated annually in the *Stocks, Bonds, Bills and Inflation (SBBI) Yearbook*, has come to be widely used in the investment world. The table "Asset Class Performance, 1926–2003" provides an overall view of how different asset classes performed over the seventy-eight-year period from 1926 through 2003. Small company stocks earned an aver-

Asset Class Performance, 1926–2003

	LARGE STOCKS	SMALL STOCKS	LONG GOV'T BONDS	T-BILLS	CPI
Annualized Return	10.4%	12.7%	5.4%	3.7%	3.0%
Annualized Standard Deviation	19.4	33.5	7.8	.89	1.87
Growth of $1	$2,286	$11,302	$61.26	$17.59	$10.52

Source: DFA Returns Program[8]

age annual compound return of 12.7 percent, large company stocks 10.4 percent, long-term government bonds 5.4 percent, and Treasury bills 3.7 percent. During this period, the annual inflation rate was 3.0 percent.

We can draw some conclusions from the above table. First, it's quite clear that stocks have widely outperformed fixed-income investments. This reveals in a dramatic way the relationship between risk and return: an investor incurring more risk gets more return and one that incurs less risk gets less return. For example, if you had invested $1 in the large company stocks of the S&P 500 on January 1, 1926, it would be worth $2,286 (assuming reinvestment of dividends and no payment of taxes) at the end of 2003. The same $1 invested in long-term government bonds would now be worth only $61, and in 30-day Treasury bills only $17. To maintain its purchasing power, $1 had to increase in value to $10. It should also be noted that small company stocks widely outperformed large company stocks. One dollar invested in small company stocks would be worth $11,302 at the end of 2003, compared with $2,286 if you had invested in large company stocks. The asset classes that comprise financial markets performed well during this time period, which included periods of major crises as well as boom times.

The importance of the CRSP database cannot be overstated. Sinquefield, now co-chairman of the investment firm Dimensional Fund Advisors, has this to say about the original CRSP database: "If I had to rank events, I would say this one is probably slightly more significant than the creation of the universe...the entire field of finance has been changed and developed through that database." The CRSP database is the literal "lifeline" between academic research and the investing public. The research that relies on this database allows investors to better understand and appreciate the relationship between risk and return. This makes it easier for investors to analyze different investment strategies and gives them the opportunity to separate the good ones from the bad ones; investors would literally be "in the dark" without the CRSP database. Investors should be aware that this database is used in all the more prestigious academic studies that examine the behavior of financial markets.

The Random Walk Theory (1964)

Harry Markowitz, as noted, is credited within the academic world for creating the field of financial economics in 1952 with publication of his article, "Portfolio Selection." This field expanded to include the Random Walk Theory in 1964. In that year, a collection of articles was published in a book called *The Random Character of Stock Prices.*[9] One of the articles was a reprint of a seventy-page Ph.D. dissertation written *in 1900* by Louis Bachelier, an unknown French mathematician.[10] Bachelier was the first to observe that past movements in the price of a particular security (or even the price of the entire stock market) cannot be used to predict accurately any future changes in such prices. He concluded, as a result of statistical and mathematical reasoning, that it was impossible to predict a given future movement in the price of a security since the probability was equal that the next move in that price would be either up or down.

Subsequent studies corroborated Bachelier's findings. For example, Paul Samuelson, who in 1970 became a recipient of the Nobel Prize in Economics and was one of the most influential economists of the twentieth century, became an early adherent to Bachelier's observation. Samuelson wrote, "I shall deduce a fairly sweeping theorem in which next period's price differences are shown to be uncorrelated with (if not completely independent of) previous period's price differences."[11] Samuelson concluded that the market price of a security at any given time is the best estimate of its true value and that any short-term future changes in that price occur randomly. He agreed with Bachelier that the stock market was essentially a "random walk."

It is important to understand that the notion of "randomness" does *not* mean that the prices of stocks comprising a financial market change for no apparent reason. Rather, they change for very rational reasons in response to new unexpected information about them that continually appears in the market. In fact, it would be *irrational* for the price of a stock not to change as a result of new (hence unexpected) information that appears about the stock in the marketplace.

The Random Walk Theory was popularized by Princeton University economics professor Burton Malkiel in his book, *A Random Walk Down Wall Street* (1973). (I recommend that it be read by all fiduciaries and those that advise them, as well as individual investors.) In his book, Malkiel discusses how an investor can actually profit from the Random Walk Theory and avoid making many of the same mistakes that lead to poor investment performance, such as that identified by the DALBAR study cited in the introduction of this book. He argues that predicting future changes in the prices of stocks in attempts to profit from stock picking is foolhardy. Instead, Malkiel suggested that investors should own all stocks that comprise the stock market: "Fund spokesmen are quick to point out you can't buy the market averages. It's time the public could." Those that agreed with Malkiel's recommendation were not able to actually follow it until 1976 when Vanguard's legendary founder, John C. Bogle, established the first index fund—the Vanguard 500 Index Trust—open to retail investors. At the end of 2003, this fund was the largest stock fund in the world with approximately $72 billion in assets, growing from its initial 1976 public offering of only $11.4 million.

It is important to understand that the Random Walk Theory is essentially a reiteration of what Alfred Cowles III concluded in the early 1930s: those claiming the ability to forecast the direction of the next move in the stock market (or even a given stock) are *really just guessing.* Although there will always be those that can demonstrate superior stock-picking and market-timing abilities, you can never know *in advance* who they will turn out to be. That explains why there is little academic evidence to support the idea that stock picking or market timing can be accomplished consistently.

The lack of such evidence is a direct assault on the way that Wall Street does business. For example, technical analysis—which is an investment approach that examines past movements in securities prices to predict future movements in securities prices—is rendered worthless by the Random Walk Theory. This makes the Random Walk Theory a large target for its critics.

The Efficient Market Theory (1965)

The field of financial economics further expanded to include the Efficient Market Theory. This theory was set forth in an article by economist Eugene F. Fama in 1965.[12] Fama explained the meaning of market efficiency: "An 'efficient' market is defined as a market where there are large numbers of rational, profit-maximizers actively competing, with each trying to predict future market values of individual securities, and where important current information is almost freely available to all participants. In an efficient market, competition among the many intelligent participants leads to a situation where, at any given point in time, actual prices of individual securities already reflect the effects of information based both on events that have already occurred and on events which, as of now, the market expects to take place in the future. In other words, in an efficient market at any point in time the actual price of a security will be a good estimate of its intrinsic value."

The Efficient Market Theory has been brought into the mainstream of modern prudent fiduciary investing by the Restatement. Reporter's General Note on Restatement Section 227 notes:[13] "Economic evidence shows that, from a typical investment perspective, the major capital markets of this country are highly efficient, in the sense that available information is rapidly digested and reflected in the market prices of securities. As a result, fiduciaries and other investors are confronted with potent evidence that the application of expertise, investigation, and diligence in efforts to 'beat the market' in these publicly traded securities ordinarily promises little or no payoff, or even a negative payoff after taking account of research and transaction costs. Empirical research supporting the theory of efficient markets reveals that in such markets skilled professionals have rarely been able to identify underpriced securities (that is, to outguess the market with respect to future return) with any regularity. In fact, evidence shows that there is little correlation between fund managers' earlier successes and their ability to produce above-market returns in subsequent periods." (See Appendix II: Subsequent Performance of Mutual Funds.)

The most significant implication of the Efficient Market Theory is that *it's very difficult for an investor (whether ama-*

teur or professional) to outperform the market over the long run, particularly on a risk-adjusted basis. This, of course, is a direct threat to the professional money management industry, which explains its fierce criticism of the Efficient Market Theory. These critics ask, for example, how a financial market can be efficient when it loses more than 20 percent of its value in one day, as happened to the stocks of the S&P 500 in the "crash" of 1987. Efficient Market Theory proponents reply that Fama said the prices of stocks at any given point in time are only a "good estimate" of their intrinsic values, not that those prices reflected *actual* intrinsic values. In other words, the current price of an investment is the best estimate, *however good or bad,* of the value of the investment. The Efficient Market Theory posits that at any given point in time, the consensus view of investors in a financial market may temporarily price securities well above or below their true values, thereby setting up the possibility for occasional market corrections such as occurred in 1987. Logically, though, no one can know for sure, until *after* the fact, whether market prices are set too high or too low! The only condition for an efficient market is that there cannot be a disproportionate number of investors profiting consistently at the expense of other investors in the market; in fact, academic evidence indicates this is the case.

Another implication of the Efficient Market Theory is that its continued validity is assured not by its proponents but by its *detractors.* Fama observed that it is the very "competition among the many intelligent participants" that creates market efficiency. Those "intelligent participants" are investors that engage in "active" investment strategies whose goal is to outperform the market through research that identifies undervalued (or overvalued) stocks. These efforts by active investors are an indication of their disbelief in the Efficient Market Theory. But those very same efforts, according to Fama, also (ironically) create an efficient market in which the prices of stocks are generally the same as their true underlying values. The collective efforts of the intelligent active investors, then, create the very condition—efficient markets—that they so heatedly deny exists. Fama does, however, make a distinction between intelligent active investors and unintelligent active investors. Unintelligent active investors may be the reason that stock prices, from time to time, are disengaged from their intrinsic values (unintelligent investors are those that display poor investor behavior).

Fiduciaries and their investment advisers need to understand and articulate the position they are taking on whether they believe some (or all) financial markets are efficient or inefficient. They should have a basic understanding of the Random Walk Theory and its central idea that it is impossible to predict a given future movement in the price of a security since there is an equal chance that the next move in that price will be either up or down. Fiduciaries and their investment advisers should also understand the most significant implication of the Efficient Market Theory: it's very difficult for investors to outperform the market over the long run, particularly on a risk-adjusted basis.

The Random Walk Theory and the Efficient Market Theory, taken together, present a logical explanation for why financial markets are efficient. They also explain why most investors cannot profit even from inefficient financial markets. These two theories form the basis for a heated argument between those that are engaged in active investment strategies who believe that financial markets are inefficient and those that are engaged in passive investment strategies who believe that financial markets are efficient. I will discuss in more detail the notion of "active" investing and "passive" investing at the beginning of Step Four. It is imperative that fiduciaries and their investment advisers have a sound understanding of these two different approaches to investing.

Chapter Two

Practical Applications

Real-world application of theories can prove to be difficult. By understanding the concepts within the Capital Asset Pricing Model (CAPM) and the Fama-French Three-Factor Model, fiduciaries can reduce this difficulty and use these tools to facilitate sound investment analysis and decision-making.

William Sharpe and the Capital Asset Pricing Model (1965)

In my discussion with Dr. Markowitz, he told me that one day in 1960 he was sitting in his office at the RAND Corporation in Santa Monica, California, when a young man named William Sharpe wandered in. Sharpe was working on his Ph.D. at UCLA and was told by his professor, Fred Weston, to visit Markowitz to see if he had any ideas for his doctoral thesis. This chance encounter is what ultimately led Sharpe to develop the Capital Asset Pricing Model, for which he eventually received the Nobel Prize in Economics.

The CAPM is a model that makes a number of assumptions about the relationship between investment risk and return. Like most asset pricing models, the CAPM makes predictions about future expected investment returns.

The CAPM is relatively simple and, once the proper inputs have been identified (which is often difficult), so is the formula used to determine the expected rate of return. That formula is:

Expected return = Risk-free return + beta (market return − risk-free return)

Beta

According to the CAPM, the degree to which the expected return of an individual stock is influenced by—or fluctuates in value relative to—the stock market is termed the stock's *beta.* Beta is the "guts" of the CAPM within the above formula. The CAPM assigns a beta of 1.0 to the stock market.[1] Each individual stock, though, has its own beta assigned to it either by financial analysts or on the basis of its past performance relative to that of the market.[2] For example, suppose that over the past five years IBM stock went up in value more than the market portfolio in a rising market and fell further in value than the market portfolio in a declining market. Further suppose that, on average, when the market portfolio went up 10 percent in value, IBM rose 12 percent in value, and when the market portfolio fell 10 percent in value, IBM fell 12 percent in value. The IBM stock therefore had a beta of 1.2, which means that it experienced 20 percent more volatility than the market portfolio in both rising and declining markets. Stocks with betas greater than 1.0 are more volatile and thus have *higher* expected returns than the market portfolio.[3] A stock's beta thus determines how much higher or lower the expected return of that stock is estimated to be relative to the expected return of the stock market as a whole.[4]

The CAPM input most commonly used for the *risk-free return* is the one-year Treasury bill.[5] In this case, the return for a Treasury bill is 1.25 percent. The CAPM input most commonly used for the *market return* is the historical return of the stock market, which in this case we assume to be 10 percent per year. To continue the example of IBM and using the following inputs for the CAPM, the expected return of IBM is determined to be 11.75 percent.

Expected return = Risk-free return + beta (market return − risk-free return)
11.75 = 1.25 + 1.2 (10.0 − 1.25)

Advisers should understand some other important work pioneered by Sharpe. He broke down the total risk in a portfolio into two different kinds of risk: uncompensated risk (also referred to as "unsystematic" risk or "nonmarket" risk) and compensated risk (also referred to as "systematic" risk or "market" risk). Uncompensated risk is the uncertainty of how news may affect the price of a particular company's stock. For example, if a meat packing company is found to have unhealthy slaughtering conditions, the price of the company's stock may fall even on a day when the overall stock market rises in price. Compensated risk is the uncertainty of how news may affect many stocks—or even all the stocks in the stock market. A good jobs report, wars, or recessions are examples of news events (both good and bad) that have the weight to move the entire stock market.

According to CAPM, the formula for total risk is defined as follows:

Total risk = Compensated risk + uncompensated risk

Investors who hold stocks must bear compensated risk. Stockholding investors can, however, reduce the uncompensated risk in their portfolios; in fact, they can eliminate nearly all of it through diversification. Modern Portfolio Theory posits that if risk can be eliminated from an investor's portfolio, then the market will not compensate the investor for carrying uncompensated risk. In short, an investor receives no benefit of additional return for bearing uncompensated risk. That's why Sharpe maintains that investors should buy and hold broadly diversified baskets of stocks. In fact, the super-efficient portfolio of Sharpe's one-factor CAPM is the market portfolio. No other portfolio with equal risk offers a higher expected return and no other portfolio with equal expected return is less risky.

Most investors are willing to accept some risk if they expect to be rewarded for doing so. Compensated risk is the only risk investors are rewarded for incurring because it cannot be diversified out of a portfolio. Examples of compensated risks are any that cannot be avoided after proper diversification of a portfolio has been employed, such as recessions, wars, structural changes in the economy, tax law changes, and inflation. Investors cannot avoid these risks if they want to be invested in the stock market. Investors can, however, avoid risks that can affect specific companies such as business, financial, and liquidity risk. In short, compensated risk is associated with broad macro events that can affect all stocks; while uncompensated risk is associated with narrower micro events that can affect specific stocks.

The table below, "Reducing Risk through Diversification," provides an example of the interplay between compensated risk

Reducing Risk through Diversification, 1994–2003

FUND NAME	1994	1995	1996	1997	1998	1999
Janus Twenty	−6.7%	36.2%	27.8%	29.7%	73.3%	64.9%
Wilshire 5000	−0.1%	36.5%	21.2%	31.2%	23.4%	23.5%

Source: Morningstar Principia

and uncompensated risk. The Janus Twenty mutual fund is a concentrated mutual fund (i.e., one with relatively few stocks invested in a narrow market sector) that is marketed as a superior performer based on the manager's skill in identifying undervalued stocks. In the late 1990s, this fund posted celebrated returns; true to form, investors poured money into it hoping to capture large returns. In fact, assets in the fund swelled from $6 billion in 1997 to more than $36 billion in 1999. The table shows the returns and standard deviations of the Janus Twenty fund compared to the Wilshire 5000 index (a broad measure of the U.S. stock market's value) for each year of the ten-year period ending December 31, 2003.

The Janus Twenty fund held thirty-four stocks (as of December 31, 2003) while the Wilshire 5000 index reflects the value of more than 6,000 stocks. The standard deviation (a measure of risk that includes both uncompensated and compensated risk) of the Janus fund was 24.9 and that of the Wilshire 5000 index was 17.8. This means that the Janus fund, as measured by standard deviation, was approximately 40 percent riskier than the index, even though the fund and the index had the same average annual return of 10.6 percent. This additional risk resulted from exposure to too much uncompensated risk. For the period

2000	2001	2002	2003	AVERAGE RETURN	10-YEAR STANDARD DEVIATION
−32.4%	−29.2%	−24.0%	25.1%	10.6%	24.9
−10.9%	−10.8%	−20.8%	31.6%	10.6%	17.8

in question, then, investors in the Janus Twenty fund failed to receive extra return because they bore uncompensated risk that could have been diversified away.

The example in the table shows the very tangible benefit—smoother portfolio performance—of reducing uncompensated risk. It is a reminder to fiduciaries that they must not only pay attention to return but to risk as well. Fiduciaries that focus solely on an investment's return and ignore its risk are at risk themselves of breaching their duties. Remember, the "central consideration" of a fiduciary as stated in the Uniform Prudent Investor Act is to make the tradeoff between portfolio risk and return.

In addition to beta, there are other statistical concepts used in the CAPM that advisers should be familiar with, such as alpha, R-squared, and the Sharpe ratio.

Alpha

One of the most popular uses of the CAPM is to evaluate portfolio performance. Hundreds of millions of dollars are spent trying to identify the best-performing mutual funds and managers. The CAPM can be used to gauge whether a particular money manager is delivering return in excess of what a particular portfolio should have earned given the risk, as measured by beta, it incurred. If the manager achieves that excess, the CAPM makes the assumption that the manager has added value—as measured by alpha—through skillful stock picking or market timing. Alpha is therefore a measure of the difference between the actual return generated by a portfolio and the return expected of that portfolio as a result of its risk exposure. In short, alpha measures investment skill.

If a money manager has a mutual fund portfolio with a beta of 1.2, for example, the CAPM forecasts that the fund's return should be 20% greater than the market portfolio. If the market goes up 10% in value, CAPM predicts the fund should be up 12% in value. If the manager earns a return of 14%, it is said that the manager provides an alpha of two percentage points (i.e., the difference between 14% and the 12% predicted by the CAPM). Note that if the market portfolio goes down 10% in value, the CAPM predicts the money manager's fund should go down 12% in value. If the return of the fund manager is down by only 10%, it is said that the manager has provided an alpha of two percentage points because the return of the fund it managed did not fall as much as the market portfolio.

The formula to calculate an alpha is:

Alpha = Excess return* − (beta (benchmark − Treasury bill rate))

*Excess return = (Fund return – Treasury bill rate)

As you can see, the formula requires plugging in two factors: beta and a benchmark return. This is a very important distinction that must be made in this discussion of how to calculate alpha: there are *two* betas and *two* benchmarks that can be used to calculate an alpha. One is the beta and return associated with a broad market index and the other is a beta and return associated with a "best fit" index. *When calculating alpha, the beta associated with the "best fit" index should be used, not the beta associated with the broad market index.* But how do you determine which "best fit" index to use? Another statistical measure with which fiduciaries should be familiar is known as *R-squared,* which helps to determine which "best fit" index is best.

R-squared

R-squared, which reflects the percentage of price movements in a mutual fund that can be attributed to movements in an index; the values of R-squared range from 0 to 1. Alpha, as noted, is a measure of the difference between the actual return generated by a portfolio and the return expected of that portfolio due to its risk exposure. If a portfolio manager invests primarily in stocks that are riskier than the broad market index, it is expected the return of that portfolio will be higher.

Note, though, that an alpha calculation comparing the returns of a riskier group of stocks to a less risky group of stocks can be misleading; it is like comparing apples to oranges. A much better solution is to compare the manager's group of risky stocks to an index of equally risky stocks (or one that is as close as possible). And that is exactly what the statistical concept of R-squared does: *it identifies an index that more closely matches the risk of the given portfolio that is being analyzed.*

As a result, it is the beta and return associated with the "best fit" index that should be used to calculate alpha, since the best fit index will have the highest R-squared. And the higher the R-squared, the more meaningful the alpha calculation will be in measuring a money manager's investment skill.

The example in the table at right, "Broad Market versus 'Best Fit' Index," demonstrates how misleading an alpha calculation can be when different betas are used in the calculation. Employing data from Morningstar, I used two different betas to calculate the alpha of the Dimensional Fund Advisors Small Cap Value mutual fund for the three-year period ending March 31, 2004.[6] When measured against the S&P 500 index, the manager of the DFA fund generates a substantial alpha of 22.10% with an R-squared of 60. When measured against the Russell 2000 Value index, which has an R-squared of 97, the manager generated an alpha of 3.47%, much less than 22.10%, but still a very significant alpha. While the fund manager would rather have an alpha of 22.10% than 3.47%, it is important to remember that the goal of using alpha is to measure accurately whether or not a manager is adding performance in excess of

Broad Market versus "Best Fit" Index: Which is Appropriate?

MORNINGSTAR	BROAD MARKET INDEX S&P 500	"BEST FIT" INDEX RUSSELL 2000 VALUE
R-squared	0.60	0.97
Beta	0.98	1.15
Alpha	22.10	3.47

Note: Data for three-year period ending March 31, 2004.

Source: Morningstar Principia

what is expected due to the risk the manager has taken. The 18.63% differential (22.10% – 3.47%) between the two alphas has nothing to do with the manager's skill but rather with the fact that the manager was rewarded for taking extra risk relative to the risk of the broad market index.

What can advisers learn from this? For one thing, they should be aware of the actual index that is used to calculate alpha; it is possible to have a negative alpha with a "best fit" index and a positive alpha with a broad market index. Advisers also should be aware of not confusing extra return that is generated by taking extra risk with extra return generated as a result of true investment skill (i.e., alpha). The former is not worth paying for, while the latter is.

Academics that specialize in statistics tell me that an alpha score associated with an index with an R-squared of less than 0.80 is not meaningful because it cannot be determined who or what is actually responsible for the excess return, whether that return is negative or positive.

Sharpe Ratio

The Sharpe ratio measures the excess return generated per unit of risk taken; this is referred to as "risk-adjusted return." The formula for the Sharpe ratio is very simple:

(Fund return – Treasury bill) / standard deviation

This calculation is more accurate and of greater benefit when it is used to compare similar types of mutual funds. For example, assume an investor decides to invest a portion of her funds in a large-cap value fund. She has narrowed her search to the following two funds in the table below, "The Sharpe Ratio." Both have the same three-year return. Which fund should she choose?

This table shows that both Fund A and Fund B had the same return, but that Fund A took less risk (i.e., standard deviation). Fund A is therefore a more efficient mutual fund because it earned 0.45 percent return for each unit of risk taken versus only 0.33 percent for Fund B.

The Sharpe Ratio

FUND NAME	3-YEAR ANNUALIZED RETURN	STANDARD DEVIATION	SHARPE RATIO*
Fund A	12%	22%	0.45
Fund B	12%	30%	0.33

*Assumes three-month Treasury bill rate of 2%

Source: Hatton Consulting, Inc.

Problems with the CAPM and Beta

A major criticism of the CAPM is that beta is not a complete measure of risk, which results in a model that has relatively poor predictive ability. For example, in 1984 small company stocks had a historical beta of approximately 1.2. During the period 1984 to 1990 the overall market returned 13.8 percent. The CAPM would have predicted that small company stocks return 16.6 percent (13.8% × 1.2) per year during that period. In fact, though, small-cap stocks actually returned only 3.9 percent per year.[7] So, even though small company stocks were riskier (as identified by a beta of 1.2) than the market as a whole, those stocks realized a return significantly *lower* than that predicted by the CAPM.

As you can see, the predictive power of the CAPM can be limited because of its reliance on only one factor: the market. That's why the CAPM does not explain very well the source of risk from which stock returns are generated. I will explore this issue in greater detail when discussing the Fama-French Three-Factor Model.

Despite the CAPM's shortcomings, it is widely accepted and used to analyze individual investments and whole portfolios. For fiduciaries, the primary concepts of the CAPM they need to understand are: compensated versus uncompensated risk, beta, alpha, R-squared, and the Sharpe ratio. A thorough familiarity with these concepts allows for high-quality investment analysis and management, which is clearly an important component to the investment process.

The Fama-French Three-Factor Model (1992)

Like the CAPM, the Fama-French Three-Factor Model is an asset-pricing model. However, there is a significant difference in the predictive quality of the two models because proponents of the Three-Factor Models believe the CAPM measures investment risk in an incomplete way. The Fama-French model improves upon the CAPM by offering a better way to measure investment risk. This allows investors to expose their portfolios to certain identifiable sources of risk that can reward them with higher investment returns.

Prior to 1992, researchers didn't have a very good idea about what sources of investment risk actually produced higher returns. They had only William Sharpe's one-factor CAPM to explain where investment returns came from. The *one factor* in Sharpe's CAPM is the *stock market.* That is, the CAPM posits that the most important determinant of investment return is the amount of a portfolio invested in the stock market.

In 1992, Eugene F. Fama of the University of Chicago and Kenneth R. French of Dartmouth College developed a three-factor model to characterize and describe the relationship between investment risk and return. Their model, essentially an extension of the one-factor CAPM, added two more fundamental determinants of investment return. Fama and French concluded that the addition of two determinants, size and value, combined with Sharpe's one determinant of investment return, the market, do the best job of pinpointing the sources of investment risk that account for higher stock returns. Fama and French referred to these three determinants—market, size, and value—as *risk factors.* They are clear in saying that risk factors are not risk per se but indicators of risk that the stock market seems to reward investors for bearing over the long run. According to the Fama-French findings, a risk factor is a "dimension" of stock returns.

The one-factor CAPM suggests that if an investor wants to build a portfolio with an expected return higher than the market return, then the portfolio must have a beta greater than 1. The Fama-French Three-Factor Model suggests that to earn a

Size and Value Return Premium

ASSET CLASS (INDEX/ ASSET CLASS FUND)	ANNUALIZED RETURN %	ANNUALIZED STANDARD DEVIATION
U.S. Large Stocks		
Fama-French Large Value	12.0	25.8
Large Cap (S&P 500)	10.4	19.5
Fama-French Large Growth	9.6	19.0
U.S. Small Stocks		
Fama-French Small Value	14.9	29.4
Small-Cap Stocks (CRSP 9-10)	13.0	33.7
Fama-French Small Growth	9.8	27.5
International Stocks (1975–2003)		
MSCI EAFE Value	13.9	16.9
MSCI EAFE ND	11.8	17.1
MSCI EAFE Growth	9.6	17.9

Source: DFA Returns Program

return in excess of the market return, an investor must build a portfolio with larger holdings of value stocks and small company stocks than are present in the market portfolio. Fama and French found that small company stocks and value stocks have higher expected returns because they are riskier than large stocks and growth stocks (I will discuss why they reached this conclusion shortly).

The table above, "Size and Value Return Premium," provides performance data on how value stocks and small company stocks have performed historically in stock markets around the world for the period January 1927–December 2003 (measurement period for international stocks is 1975–2003).

The three factors are:

- ➢ ***Market***—Stocks have higher expected returns than fixed income.
- ➢ ***Size***—Small stocks have higher expected returns than large stocks.
- ➢ ***Value***—"Value" stocks have higher expected returns than "Growth" stocks.

The Fama-French model attempts to show investors how to incrementally increase the risk in their portfolios so that they can earn potentially higher returns.

Before entering into the specifics of this model, it is important to understand a very important idea that Fama and French believe is the foundation for the higher returns generated by small company stocks and value stocks: *cost of capital,* a concept that was set forth by Merton Miller in his Nobel prize–winning research. The cost of capital to a company equals the expected return to an investor that holds the stock of that company. The cost of capital is the price that a company must pay in order to obtain money. An example may help explain this: Suppose that Microsoft and Apple each go to the bank for a loan. Which company will have to pay the higher cost of capital (i.e., the higher interest rate) on its loan? Apple will, because analysis conducted by investors, as well as bankers, have determined its current financial strength and future ability to earn sustainable profits is weaker than Microsoft's. The bank must charge Apple extra interest for taking the added potential risk that Apple won't be able to repay the bank's loan. That's why companies that are doing poorly must pay a higher interest rate on borrowed money than companies that are doing well. Likewise, the riskier the company's stock, the higher the cost of capital it must pay. If a company that incurs a higher cost of capital from a bank decides to fund operations in part by issuing stock, the prospective stockholders (who are alternatives to the bank, but essentially are doing the same thing by providing capital) will demand a higher return on their investment.

Because investors (the market) think that Apple is riskier, they drive down its stock price low enough so that its expected return is high enough to make it worthwhile for them to hold Apple stock despite the extra risk they take when buying it. In this way, stock prices adjust to reflect Apple's perceived relatively greater riskiness. This ensures that Apple's stock also will be purchased by investors, even though Microsoft has better earnings prospects and it seems generally safer to hold. Companies that are under financial distress for various reasons, then, tend to be riskier investments that offer higher expected returns. Small companies and value companies tend to experience financial difficulty more often than large companies and growth companies, which is why they have higher costs of capital *and* higher expected returns.

It's important to understand that this doesn't mean Apple will always outperform Microsoft. Don't forget: risk is uncertainty (more things can happen than will happen), and if we knew what was going to happen in the future, there wouldn't be any such thing as investment risk!

Market Risk Factor—Total Stock Market minus Treasury Bills

It is fairly easy to understand and accept that stocks are riskier than high-quality fixed-income securities such as Treasury bills. The three-factor model, as I stated, attempts to show investors how to increase incrementally the risk in their portfolios so that they can earn potentially higher returns. If an investor wishes to be completely risk-free, she can invest 100 percent of her money in 90-day Treasury bills. If she wishes to incrementally increase the risk in her portfolio, she can invest 90 percent in Treasury bills and 10 percent in a total stock market mutual fund. To further increase the risk of her portfolio in order to earn potentially higher returns, she can simply reduce the amount in Treasury bills and add more to the total stock market fund. This essentially is how investors increase their exposure to the Fama-French market-risk factor and thereby increase the expected rate of return of their portfolios. (This process also reflects the essence of the CAPM.) The Fama-French market-risk factor has provided investors with an additional 8.48 percent return per year on average over 90-day Treasury bills for about the last seventy-five years.[8]

Fama and French knew, however, that investors were not simply interested in a "market" return. Fama and French also knew that the traditional methods of trying to beat the market—stock picking and market timing—lacked academic evidence as a sustainable strategy to deliver above market returns. Their research identified two other factors, size and value, that seem to systematically reward investors with higher-than-market returns.

Size and Value Risk Factors

The size risk factor results from comparing the performance of small company stocks to large company stocks. The value risk factor results from comparing the performance of value stocks to growth stocks. (Fama and French identify value and growth by book-to-market ratio [BtM]. High BtM stocks are deemed "value" and low BtM are deemed "growth." BtM is calculated by dividing the book value of a company by its current market price.) Fama and French found that small company stocks and value stocks, as a group, experienced higher returns than large company stocks and growth stocks.[9] Seeking to understand why small company stocks and value stocks have higher expected returns, Fama and French studied the profitability of such stocks. The table at right, "Profitability versus Return," summarizes their research.

Profitability versus Return

EARNINGS VERSUS RETURNS, 1964–2002	VALUE STOCKS	GROWTH STOCKS	SMALL STOCKS	LARGE STOCKS
Earnings-to-Assets Ratio[10]	4.21	9.05	3.40	5.85
Average Returns	15.49%	10.69%	15.20%	11.47%

Source: Dimensional Fund Advisors

The Fama-French findings are counterintuitive. For the period of 1964–2002, value stocks had an earnings-to-assets ratio of 4.21, compared with a more healthy 9.05 for growth stocks. Yet the average return for value stocks far exceeded that of growth stocks, 15.49 percent to 10.69 percent, respectively. The same held true when small company stocks were compared with large company stocks. The earnings-to-assets ratio for small company stocks was 3.40, compared with 5.85 for large company stocks. Yet again, small company stocks outperformed large company stocks, 15.20 percent to 11.47 percent. Why did this happen? After all, market participants as a whole look at small company stocks and value stocks and, in effect, exclaim: "Hey, their earnings are horrible!" As a result of this collective opinion of the stock market, the prices of these stocks become *depressed;* but once that happens, their expected returns become *higher.* (This is true even though the earnings of small company stocks and value stocks are poorer relative to large company stocks and growth stocks.)

Another way of looking at this counterintuitive outcome is to think about the relationship between risk and return. Investors agree that investments perceived to be safer would have lower expected returns than investments perceived to be riskier. Take our Microsoft and Apple example. Which company is perceived to be safer? Most would agree that it would be Microsoft. So, if risk and return are related, Microsoft's expected return will be lower than Apple's. To understand why expected returns for small company stocks and value stocks are higher than those of large company stocks and growth stocks, it may come down to asking which stocks are "safer" and which are "riskier."

An interesting study conducted by Michelle Clayman supports Fama and French's findings that value stocks provide higher returns than growth stocks.[11] Clayman based her study on the best-seller, *In Search of Excellence,* by Tom Peters and Bob Waterman. Peters and Waterman studied twenty-nine companies that had excellent records in such areas as profitability and how they treated their employees. Clayman dubbed these companies to be "excellent." She then created a virtual mutual fund of these companies and named it the "Excellent Company" portfolio. Clayman also created a portfolio made of the stocks of companies that had terrible profitability measures and poor reputations for how they treated their employees. (Such stocks would be like the "riskier" stocks identified by Fama and French's findings.) Clayman called this the "Unexcellent Company" portfolio.

The Clayman study found that the value (unexcellent) stocks outperformed the growth (excellent) stocks, 298 percent to 182 percent, over the five-year period of 1981–1985. This meant that investors earned higher returns by owning the stocks of companies with poor earnings and bad management. While this conclusion may seem counterintuitive, it's reasonable to expect that investors require a higher return to compensate them for the greater risk of holding what are perceived to be the stocks of "unexcellent" companies. But investors still tend to think that stocks issued by healthy companies are better investments than stocks issued by sickly companies. After all, if you ask someone for a stock tip, you want to hear about the next Microsoft, not a stock with distressed earnings. In fact, though, you should be interested in great *investments* (i.e., value stocks), not great *companies* (i.e., growth stocks).

It is very important to understand that small company stocks and value stocks don't always outperform large company stocks and growth stocks. The following two tables, "Inconsistency of Return Premium" and "Large Value Stocks versus Large-Cap Stocks," show this.

The table below shows that the size risk factor is unpredictable. The cycle of good or bad returns for small company stocks vis-à-vis large company stocks can last for *many years.* For example, during the seven-year period of 1977–1983, small company stocks widely outperformed large company stocks, 27.9% to 11.8%, while during the seven-year period of 1984–1990, small company stocks significantly underperformed large company stocks, 2.6% to 14.6% per year. For the thirteen-year period of 1991–2003, small company stocks again produced higher returns per year than large company stocks, 17.9% to 12.1%, respectively. However, for the entire period of 1927–2003, small company stocks returned 12.9% per year compared with 10.4% per year for large company stocks.

Inconsistency of Return Premium

PERIOD	SMALL STOCKS	LARGE STOCKS
January 1977–December 1983	27.9%	11.8%
January 1984–December 1990	2.6%	14.6%
January 1991–December 2003	17.9%	12.1%
January 1926–December 2003	12.9%	10.4%

Note: Small stocks: CRSP® 9-10, Jan. 26–Dec. 1981; DFA Micro cap, Jan. 1982–2003. Large stocks: S&P 500, Jan. 26–Dec. 2003.

Source: DFA Returns Program; and Center for Research in Security Prices. Used with permission.

Large Value Stocks versus Large-Cap Stocks, 1963–2003

ROLLING TIME PERIODS	1-YEAR
Number of Periods	475
Periods in Which Large Value Outperformed Large Cap	306
Percentage of Periods in Which Large Value Outperformed Large Cap	64%

Source: Dimensional Fund Advisors

The table "Large Value Stocks versus Large-Cap Stocks" shows the percentage of time during the period of 1963–2003 that value stocks outperformed large company stocks as measured by the S&P 500.

The table above shows that in the 475 one-year rolling periods since 1963, value stocks outperformed the S&P 500 64 percent of the time. As the rolling periods lengthen, value stocks tend to outperform more frequently. Fama and French have never suggested that any of the risk factors manifest themselves year in and year out. In fact, Fama and French have said it can take *decades* for the risk premiums of small company stocks and value stocks to be realized.

The key to understanding the connection between the size and value risk factors, and stock returns, then, lies ultimately in focusing on the relative price of a stock. As the price of a stock falls relative to its book value, its book-to-market ratio rises and its market capitalization relative to all other stocks falls. This happens because these stocks have poor earnings and exhibit other indications of financial distress. That makes these stocks riskier in the collective eyes of the market. At some point the stock price relative to its book value is priced to induce investors to purchase it.

3-YEAR	5-YEAR	10-YEAR	15-YEAR	20-YEAR
451	427	367	307	247
317	313	279	240	220
70%	73%	76%	78%	89%

The practical uses of the Fama-French Three-Factor Model can be put to use in the following ways to benefit advisers and fiduciaries.

Use No. 1: Structure Portfolios to Increase Expected Returns

The three-factor model provides investors a framework in which to construct portfolios that have higher expected returns than the market. How a portfolio is structured for exposure to the three risk factors—that is, what asset classes it holds and in what proportions—determines how well the portfolio performs relative to other portfolios. The "structure decision" —i.e., the degree of exposure to the three risk factors—is therefore the most crucial decision because it accounts for nearly all the returns earned by stocks. In short, *structure determines the vast majority of stock returns.* The graph on the following page, "Dimensions of Stock Returns," shows how portfolios are positioned based on their exposure to the three risk factors.

The place where a portfolio is positioned (i.e., structured) on the "cross-hair" map in the graph determines the vast majority of its return. The cross-hair map has two dimensions: the size dimension is plotted along the vertical axis and the value dimension is plotted along the horizontal axis. The axes represent

Dimensions of Stock Returns

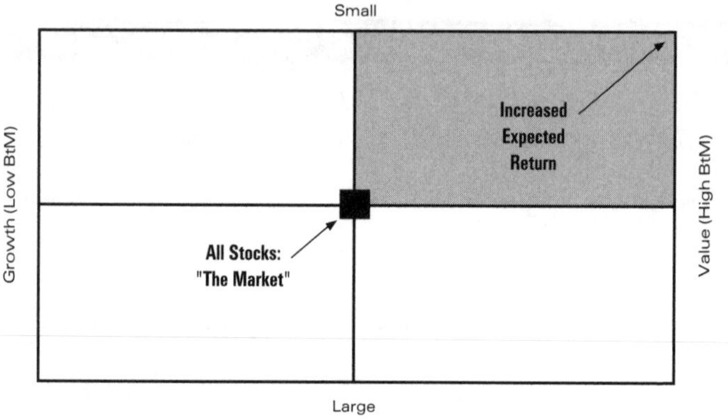

Source: Dimensional Fund Advisors

Increasing Risk through Portfolio Structure (April 1993–July 2004)

ASSET CLASS	PORTFOLIO 1	PORTFOLIO 2	PORTFOLIO 3	PORTFOLIO 4
S&P 500	100	80	70	60
Large Value Stocks		20	20	30
Micro-Cap Stocks			10	10
Small Value Stocks				
Annualized Returns	**9.99**	**10.35**	**10.87**	**11.04**
Annualized Standard Deviation	**14.98**	**14.78**	**14.62**	**14.60**

Source: DFA Returns Program

exposures to these two risk factors. Portfolios that take on a lot of the size risk factor appear farther up the vertical size axis and portfolios that take on much of the value risk factor appear farther right on the horizontal value axis. The crosshair map doesn't have a separate axis for the market risk factor because all stock portfolios have similar market risk. All stock portfolios are therefore positioned relative to the stock market, which sits right at the cross hairs of the map. The table below, "Increasing Risk through Portfolio Structure," sets up an example of how portfolios can be structured with varying degrees of exposure to the three factors. The annualized returns and standard deviations are for the period April 1993 through July 2004.

Moving from portfolio 1 to 10, you can see how the percentage of small company stocks and value stocks increases incrementally. This movement also reveals that an increasing exposure to small company stocks and value stocks results in

PORTFOLIO 5	PORTFOLIO 6	PORTFOLIO 7	PORTFOLIO 8	PORTFOLIO 9	PORTFOLIO 10
50	40	30	20	10	
30	30	30	30	30	30
10	20	20	20	20	20
10	10	20	30	40	50
11.60	**12.07**	**12.60**	**13.12**	**13.61**	**14.10**
14.54	**14.71**	**14.89**	**15.18**	**15.57**	**16.06**

Charting Exposure to Risk

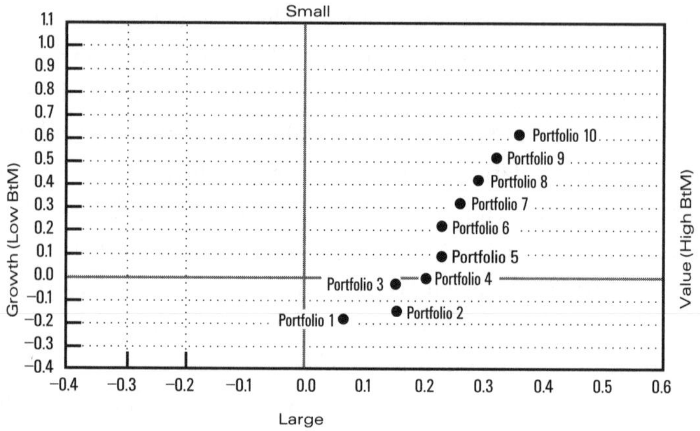

Source: Dimensional Fund Advisors

higher returns—and greater risk (i.e., standard deviation). The figure above, "Charting Exposure to Risk," shows how the ten portfolios would look plotted on a regression chart.

According to Fama and French, advisers that focus on structuring portfolios through selected exposure to the three risk factors would seem to be engaged in an activity that is more useful than attempting to pick stocks and time markets.

Use No. 2: Changing the Definition of Alpha The Fama-French model changes the definition of *alpha*. According to the one-factor CAPM, alpha is the amount by which an active money manager outperforms a market benchmark index. But the Fama-French Three-Factor Model defines alpha much more precisely. According to that model, alpha is the return that a manager achieves above the sum of the portfolio's expected return due to all three risk factors.

Alpha within the Three-Factor Model

MORNINGSTAR MARCH 31, 2004	BROAD MARKET INDEX S&P 500	"BEST FIT" INDEX RUSSELL 2000 VALUE	FAMA-FRENCH INDEX
R-squared	60	97	0.91
Beta	0.98	1.15	0.80
Alpha	22.10	3.47	0.01

Source: Morningstar Principia and DFA Returns Program

According to the Fama-French model, then, alpha measures the manager's skill in earning a return that couldn't have been achieved by indexing the same risk exposure in the portfolio run by the manager. In short, did the active money manager earn anything above the index return? For example, the table "Broad Market versus 'Best Fit' Index" (page 47) now has had added to it a fourth column, as seen in the table above, "Alpha within the Three-Factor Model," showing that under the Fama-French model the alpha for the DFA Small Value fund is zero.

The Fama-French model says that the job of a money manager isn't to earn additional returns that are compensation for incurring extra compensated risk; rather it is to *earn additional returns that can't be achieved through indexing.* And this is exactly what a manager's alpha is in the three-factor model. So, what shows up as alpha (i.e., skill) in the one-factor CAPM may be nothing more than a measurement error. Put another way, many active managers who are credited with alpha under CAPM have really only been systematically subjecting their clients to two risk factors, size and value, which have allowed them to earn their alphas. Therefore, if an investor compares the performances of active managers between CAPM and the Fama-French model, he may see radical changes in the outcomes.

Use No. 3: Style Analysis It is possible to use the three-factor model to identify where specific money managers fall on the cross-hair map. This is quite important because managers have a tendency to shift their style, which in turn can negatively affect the desired asset allocation. The figure below, "Analyzing Style Drift," shows where three popular mutual funds plotted on the cross-hair map for two periods, January 1970–March 1987 and April 1987–July 2004. You can see how some of the portfolios shifted over time; even though the names of the funds are the same, they became very different portfolios when moving from one time period to the next. Fiduciaries should look for consistency in investment style over long periods of time; three-factor analysis can help.

Analyzing Style Drift

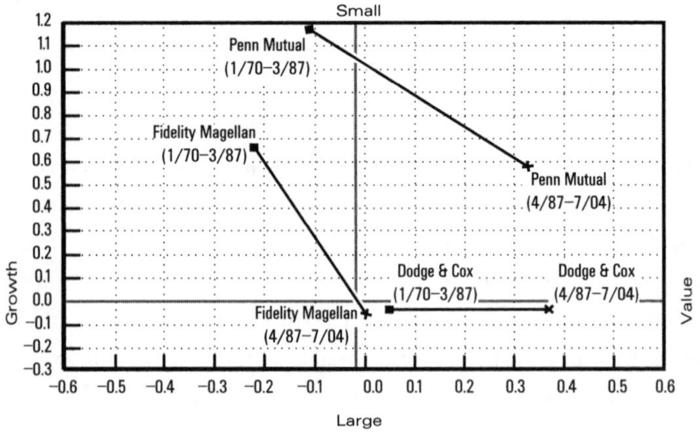

Source: DFA Returns Program

Use No. 4: Investing in Foreign Stocks The size and value risk factors Fama and French found in the U.S. stock market are also present in other stock markets outside the United States. From 1975 to 1996, for example, these factors were apparent in eleven of twelve major stock markets, including the United Kingdom, Japan, and Germany. (The Italian stock market was the only one in which book-to-market did not appear to be used; however, the risk factors were apparent using other measures of value.) The two risk factors also are present in less well-developed markets (i.e., emerging markets).

The fact that the risk factors uncovered by the Fama-French findings have been identified in many other stock markets the world over provides more evidence of the validity of the model.

Although there is credible evidence that the two risk factors are present in markets around the world, there is disagreement about the reason small stocks and value stocks deliver higher returns. Are the higher returns of small and value stocks the result of mispricing in an inefficient market, or compensated risk in an efficient market? Few dispute the higher returns of small and value stocks. Criticism of the Fama-French Three-Factor Model centers on whether the superior performance of small company stocks and value stocks is the result of market inefficiencies or whether the time period of the outperformance is an anomaly that won't reappear in the future. Fama and French are convinced that the return premiums of small company stocks and value stocks are the result of market rewards for compensated risk and that these rewards will continue through time. Only time and future research can settle this score.

The Fama-French Three-Factor Model is theory. There is much statistical evidence supporting the idea that small and value stocks offer higher expected returns than their large and growth counterparts. I do believe there is much merit to the theory and that it warrants fiduciaries' attention. If you do apply this theory to portfolio construction, there is ample evidence to defend the reasons for doing so, and this makes following its principles prudent.

Modern Portfolio Theory Summary

The primary goal for many investors is to achieve the greatest return for a given level of risk or the least amount of risk for a given level of return. The best way of achieving this goal, in my opinion, is to use the investment tools that have been developed on the basis of the principles of Modern Portfolio Theory. It is important for fiduciaries (as well as those that advise them) to understand that these principles also form the underpinning for all modern, prudent fiduciary investing. There are those that are critical of Modern Portfolio Theory. Most, if not all, of these critics are threatened by the findings of Modern Portfolio Theory because it directly challenges their claims that they can provide superior investment performance. In fact, my personal experience has been that money managed in accordance with the principles of Modern Portfolio Theory generates far better performance than money managed without regard to such principles.

PART TWO

The Five Steps and Twenty-Seven Practices

Step One

Analyze Current Position

Practices 1.1–1.6

Effective fiduciary investing begins with a complete understanding of an investor's current status, needs, and requirements. One of the first things you must determine, then, is the kind of investor you will be working with.

As noted in the introduction, there are six primary kinds of investors: (1) corporate retirement plans (defined benefit and defined contribution); (2) public employee retirement plans; (3) Taft-Hartley labor union retirement plans; (4) foundations/endowments/charitable trusts; (5) private trusts; and (6) individual and family accounts. I recommend that you become familiar with the legislation and the regulatory oversight bodies concerning each kind of investor. The table on the following page, "Legislation and Oversight Bodies of Investor Groups" (identical to the table on page 17) identifies different kinds of investors, the legislation that governs their investment activities, and the oversight bodies that enforce such provisions.

The five-step process and the particular Practices associated with each step that have been developed by the Foundation for Fiduciary Studies are derived from ERISA and the foregoing model acts. It is incumbent on all professional investment advis-

Legislation and Oversight Bodies of Investor Groups

INVESTOR GROUPS	LEGISLATION	OVERSIGHT BODY
Corporate Retirement Plans	ERISA	DOL, IRS, and PBGC
Public Retirement Plans	UMPERSA	State Attorney General
Taft-Hartley Plans	ERISA	PBGC, DOL, and IRS
Foundations/Endowments	UPIA	State Attorney General
Private Trusts	UPIA	State Courts
Individual and Family[1]		

Note: DOL: Department of Labor; IRS: Internal Revenue Service; PBGC: Pension Benefit Guaranty Corporation; ERISA: Employee Retirement Income Security Act; UPIA: Uniform Prudent Investor Act; UMPERSA: Uniform Management of Public Employee Retirement Systems Act.

Source: Foundation for Fiduciary Studies

ers to gain a good understanding of the twenty-seven Practices that I describe and explain in this book.

It is important to note that the Practices are guidelines—that there is no absolutely right or wrong way to fulfill the responsibilities of each Practice. There are many sources that tell advisers and the fiduciaries they serve what they should do, but there are none to my knowledge that show them how actually to implement and execute their required duties. What follows, then, is a description of the Practices and the way in which I implement and execute them within my own investment advisory practice.

Practice 1.1: *Investments are managed in accordance with applicable laws, trust documents, and written investment policy statements.*

Because the scope of this book does not allow for a detailed discussion of each piece of legislation listed in the table "Legislation and Oversight Bodies of Investor Groups," I have described them only briefly. You should, however, have a good familiarity with the governing law that applies to the kind of investor that you will be working with. For example, if you are working with 401(k) plans, you should be familiar with ERISA statutes; if you are working with private trusts, you should be familiar with the version of the Uniform Prudent Investor Act that is applicable in your particular state.

So you should begin the five-step investment management process by collecting the following documents (in many situations, you will find that some of these documents do not even exist; this is an automatic red flag):

- ➢ Applicable trust documents
- ➢ Custodial and/or brokerage statements
- ➢ Investment performance reports
- ➢ Service agreements with investment management vendors
- ➢ Investment policy statements
- ➢ Minutes of committee meetings (qualified retirement plans)
- ➢ Most recent asset allocation study
- ➢ Due-diligence files on funds and/or money managers
- ➢ Monitoring procedures for funds and/or money managers

Once all (or some) of this material has been collected, you should obtain answers to the following questions:

➢ *Do trust documents or statutes restrict or prohibit certain asset classes?* Section 4 of the UPIA states: "Within a reasonable time after accepting a trusteeship or receiving trust assets, a trustee shall review the trust assets and make and implement decisions concerning the retention and disposition of assets, in order to bring the trust portfolio into compliance with the purposes, terms, distribution requirements and other circumstances of the trust, and with the requirements of this Act." (It's important to note that if the terms of a trust document are in conflict with the UPIA on a particular issue, the trust prevails. If the trust instrument is silent on a particular issue, the provisions of the UPIA control.)

➢ *Do trust documents identify trustees and named fiduciaries?*

➢ *Is the investment committee appointed, in writing?*

➢ *If so, is there sufficient detail identifying selection criteria, duties, and responsibilities of investment committee members?*

➢ *Do trust documents allow for the fiduciaries to delegate prudently investment decisions to others?*

➢ *What are the anticipated cash flows of the portfolio over the next five years?*

➢ *What are the goals and objectives of the investor?*

In addition to the above, the following items need to be collected for these specific investor groups.

For ***defined contribution plans***, you should collect the following reports and information:

➢ Plan document

➢ Participant education material

➢ Enrollment meetings

➢ Loan activity

➢ IRS form 5500, including schedules

➢ Independent accountant's audit report (if more than 100 employees)

➢ Summary plan description

For ***defined benefit plans***, you should collect the following reports and information:

- ➢ Plan document
- ➢ IRS form 5500, including schedules
- ➢ Independent accountant's audit report (if more than 100 employees)
- ➢ Summary plan description
- ➢ Actuarial report showing Projected Benefit Obligation (PBO) and Accumulated Benefit Obligation (ABO) and assumptions used for interest rate, return, and benefit increases

For ***foundations***, ***endowments, and charitable trusts***, you should collect the following reports and information:

- ➢ Mission-based/socially responsible investment strategy
- ➢ Equilibrium spending rate (ESR); ESR = modeled return – inflation – investment expenses
- ➢ Funding support ratio (FSR); FSR = grants/operating budget of recipients
- ➢ Smoothing rules:
  —Moving average over three years
  —Preset amount over previous year (inflation-adjusted)
  —Judging the need

For ***private trusts and individual and family accounts***, you should collect the following reports and information:

- ➢ Tax returns
- ➢ Trust documents
- ➢ Complete asset/liability study
- ➢ Family tree
- ➢ Estate and philanthropic objectives, in addition to all other goals and objectives
- ➢ Five-year cash flow in/cash flow out estimate

Detailed "data gathering" questionnaires include questions about risk tolerance, expected returns, inflation rates, and so on. For the most part, investors do not really understand these questions. Therefore, I strongly recommend advisers spend time carefully discussing these types of questions with investors. A wealth of knowledge about the investor will surface, which should help to manage the assets more effectively.

Practice 1.2: *Fiduciaries are aware of their duties and responsibilities.*

It may seem curious, but it is common for fiduciaries to be unaware of their fiduciary status, let alone their responsibilities associated with that status. Advisers can provide a valuable service by making sure that fiduciaries are aware of both these aspects. The following is a reiteration of the ways in which a person (or even a committee) may acquire fiduciary status:

- ➢ Manages property for the benefit of another (corporate officers and directors, investment committee members and their assignors, trustees of private trusts);
- ➢ Exercises discretionary authority or control over assets (money managers, custodians, investment advisers); and
- ➢ Acts in a professional capacity of trust and renders comprehensive and continuous advice (investment consultants, accountants, attorneys, actuaries).

The primary duty of a fiduciary is to *manage* the overall investment process. This duty includes seven fundamental responsibilities:

- ➢ Know standards, laws, and trust provisions
- ➢ Diversify assets to specific risk/return profile of client
- ➢ Prepare investment policy statement

- ➢ Use "prudent experts" (money managers) and document due diligence
- ➢ Control and account for investment expenses
- ➢ Monitor money managers and service vendors
- ➢ Avoid conflicts of interest and prohibited transactions

It is a common belief that fiduciaries can eliminate their duties by hiring certain service providers such as money managers and investment consultants. *While fiduciaries can reduce their liability in certain situations, they cannot ever abdicate their duty to monitor the overall investment process for which they are always responsible.* The preceding seven responsibilities encompass that investment process. The following twenty-five Practices detail how to successfully execute those seven fundamental responsibilities.

Practice 1.3: *Fiduciaries and parties in interest are not involved in self-dealing.*

With respect to a retirement plan, the following are "parties in interest" under ERISA:

1) Any fiduciary, counsel, or employee of the plan;

2) A person providing services to the plan;

3) An employer any of whose employees are covered by the plan and any direct or indirect owner of 50 percent or more of such employer;

4) A relative—that is a spouse, ancestor, lineal descendant, or spouse of a lineal descendant of any of the persons described above in (1), (2), or (3);

5) An employee organization, any of whose members are covered by the plan;

6) A corporation, partnership, estate, or trust of which at least 50 percent is owned by any person or organization described above in (1), (2), (3), (4), or (5);

7) Officers, directors, 10 percent or more shareholders and employees of any person or organization described above in (2), (3), (4), (5), or (6); and

8) A 10 percent or more partner of, or joint venture with, any person or organization described in (2), (3), (5), or (6) above.

The significance of this issue is that any fiduciary that deals with a party in interest may be entering into a "prohibited transaction"—which are red flags for the Department of Labor (DOL) and will be heavily scrutinized. Even if a fiduciary believes an investment opportunity is sound and offers a better return than other appropriate investments, the DOL has made it clear this transaction should be avoided. For instance, assume $100,000 of a retirement plan's assets are invested in government bonds earning 5 percent with an approximate maturity of five years. The accountant (clearly a party in interest because he is performing a service to the plan) who performs the annual audit for the plan approaches the investment committee asking to borrow $100,000 at an 8 percent return and will collateralize the loan with a free and clear parcel of real estate that has appraised at $200,000. Earning 8 percent instead of 5 percent on a well-collateralized loan certainly seems to be in the best interest of the plan participants. It does not matter; this is a prohibited transaction and should not be entered into. Another area of concern regarding prohibited transactions and one the DOL remains on high alert for is self-dealing. An employer who sponsors a retirement plan can never use plan assets for business or any other purposes. For example, the DOL will not tolerate the employer using the money for only one or two days to make some kind of payment, such as making payroll. These are examples of transactions that are "per se" prohibited by ERISA, which means under no circumstances are the transactions permitted.

There are some exemptions to prohibited transactions; in other words certain types of transactions are not prohibited, per se. For example, at first glance the accountant from the example above would not be able to enter into an agreement to perform another service different from the audit work because, as peculiar as it seems, he is a party in interest. However, if three conditions are met—the service is necessary, the contract is reasonable, and the compensation is reasonable—then the exemption applies and the accountant can provide the additional service.

However, this can be confusing. There are certain transactions that are absolutely prohibited and some that may be allowed if certain conditions are met. If you are a plan sponsor and are even minimally unsure about entering into an agreement with a particular party I recommend seeking advice from a qualified ERISA attorney.

Below are a few other examples of conflicts of interest and self-dealing that fiduciaries should avoid:

- A plan sponsor that uses plan assets to buy real estate for corporate use
- Using assets of a private trust as collateral for loans to related parties of the trustee
- Trustee selling trust property below fair market value
- Buying artwork and/or other collectibles with trust assets for the sole purpose of putting them on display (non-investment purposes)

Practice 1.4: *Service agreements and contracts are in writing and do not contain provisions that conflict with fiduciary standards of care.*

Fiduciaries may or may not possess the entire range of skills necessary to ensure prudent investment of portfolio assets. If they do not possess such skills, they have a *duty to delegate* certain investment and management functions they have to prudent experts. Hiring professional investment advisers and/or money managers is a common way of doing this. In some instances a corporate trustee, third-party administrator, and record keepers (for retirement plans) may be needed for the management of assets. Any agreement with these or other investment professionals should be *in writing* and stipulate very clearly the scope of services to be provided, the compensation to be paid, and the length of time the service is to be provided.

One of the most confusing and ambiguous issues in managing investment assets involves commissions and fees that are paid to stockbrokers and investment advisers. For example, shares of mutual funds come in different classes: A, B, C, D, F, R, and I. There are also no-load and load mutual funds, up-front load and back-end load mutual funds, break points, and a myriad of other compensation schemes.

It is especially important to define *who* is paying the investment adviser. For example, is the adviser being compensated solely by the client? Or is the adviser receiving commissions and incentives (such as trips or other gifts) from their broker-dealer, third-party money manager, or mutual fund that the adviser is recommending? If the latter is the case, conflicts of interest may exist and must be disclosed.

I recommend the fiduciary prepare a three-column summary sheet that identifies (1) all parties involved in the management of portfolio assets; (2) the services they will provide; and (3) the specific cost for each of those services.

Practice 1.5: *There is documentation to show timing and distribution of cash flows and the payment of liabilities.*

A detailed study of cash inflows and cash outflows must be conducted, except in the case of a participant-directed retirement plan. This is so because these plans do not make systematic distributions. This helps determine whether the portfolio has ample liquidity; it also helps identify an appropriate portfolio risk level (which is discussed in detail in Practice 2.1). It is preferable to conduct a cash flow study that covers a five-year (or longer) period.

Practice 1.6: *Assets are within the jurisdiction of U.S. courts and are protected from theft and embezzlement.*

A fiduciary has the responsibility to safeguard assets under its care. This is made much easier if the assets are kept within the purview of the U.S. judicial system. That gives the government the ability to seize the assets if it is in the interests of the trust beneficiaries.

Assets should be placed with a reputable custodian. The custodian should be in compliance with governmental mandates, be up to date with all filings with the SEC and offer comprehensive asset insurance, including Securities Investor Protection Corporation (SIPC). For ERISA-qualified retirement plans, the U.S. Department of Labor requires them to maintain a surety bond in the amount of 10 percent of a plan's assets. The bond covers losses caused by the dishonest acts of plan fiduciaries. In addition, ERISA bonding requirements extend to all people who handle plan money.

An exception to the above is for advisers managing the personal assets of an individual client that has established an offshore account; this is typically done to legally shelter assets from creditors. It is assumed that federal laws will continue to impose strict reporting and tracking requirements of foreign banks and offshore trusts.[2]

Step Two

Diversify—Allocate Portfolio

Practices 2.1–2.5

The ultimate decision of this step is decide how much money is to be invested in cash, fixed income, and equity investments. Furthermore, determining the appropriate sub-asset classes of the portfolio is achieved as well. Identifying the particular investment vehicles for each asset class will be discussed in Practice 4.4.

Practice 2.1: *A risk level has been identified.*

Investment risk is a highly complex subject that includes objective measurements and subjective judgments. An example of a subjective judgment involves identifying a client's *risk tolerance,* which is the amount of *negative* change an investor can cope with with respect to the value of his portfolio. I am a strong believer that investors should take on the *least* amount of risk possible to reach their goals and objectives. The goal therefore should be to reduce the potential negative outcomes to the greatest extent possible—and in some cases to even eliminate them completely.

Identifying risk tolerance is ultimately identifying the overall "split" (i.e., allocation) of assets between growth (including stocks and other higher risk investments) and fixed-income investments consistent with the investor's investment time horizon. This requires guiding the investor through the process of development of their goals and objectives, which was done in Step One. You then need to determine what I refer to as the "target rate of return" (TRR). The TRR is the return the investor's portfolio needs to earn to accomplish the investor's goals and objectives.

The TRR can be equated to the investor's *need* to take risk. For example, assume an investor has a $1 million portfolio and would like to generate $40,000 a year adjusted for 3 percent inflation. In this example, the 7 percent TRR is simply the sum of the assumed return, 4 percent, and the assumed inflation rate, 3 percent.[1] The question then arises: What asset allocation will deliver a 7 percent return with the least amount of risk? This question is often answered through the use of a sophisticated tool called portfolio optimization software, which was developed as a result of the work done by Nobel laureate Harry Markowitz. Once certain inputs are made to this software such as desired return or risk (standard deviation), it generates an "efficient" portfolio allocation on an asset class basis. The asset allocations in the table at right, "Unconstrained Portfolio Optimization," were derived using this software. The first portfolio was generated as a result of inputting a desired return of 7 percent and the second portfolio was generated as a result of inputting a desired risk level (standard deviation) of 8 percent.

There are a number of problems with portfolio optimization software. The first problem, shown in the table, is that the asset allocations generated by the software can be somewhat unrealistic. In this example, I let the software create the asset allocations *without any constraints* as to what asset classes to consider or what minimum or maximum amounts to be invested in any asset class. For example, a 0.03 percent allocation to government bonds in Portfolio B will have no material impact on the return of that

Unconstrained Portfolio Optimization

PORTFOLIO A		PORTFOLIO B	
Desired Return	**7%**	**Desired Standard Deviation**	**8%**
Expected Standard Deviation	**5.37%**	**Expected Return**	**8.59%**

ASSET CLASS	% ALLOCATION	ASSET CLASS	% ALLOCATION
T-Notes/CD's	21.49	Intermediate Gov't Bonds	26.72
Intermediate Gov't Bonds	37.76	Long Gov't Bonds	0.03
High-Yield Bonds	4.24	High-Yield Bonds	10.16
Large Value Stocks	9.09	Large Value Stocks	18.51
Large Growth Stocks	6.98	Small Value Stocks	7.78
Small Value Stocks	1.02	Small Growth Stocks	1.91
Small Growth Stocks	2.05	Mid-Cap Stocks	2.48
Real Estate	0.78	Futures/Commodities	6.18
Futures/Commodities	4.28	Venture Capital	1.65
Venture Capital	0.64	International Stocks	8.42
International Stocks	4.22	International Bonds	16.18
International Bonds	7.48		

Source: Hatton Consulting, Inc.

portfolio, regardless of how that asset class performs. Also, for both portfolios a small allocation is made to venture capital. Most investors do not know what venture capital is, let alone understand the issues of finding a vehicle that invests in venture capital.

The second problem involves expected returns. There are two primary ways to estimate future rates of return: the historical method and the risk premium method. The historical method is a very easy estimate to make: simply use the historical returns for the various asset classes. The problem, though, is that we know history never repeats itself precisely, so any software input using the historical method of estimating future rates of return is of limited use. The risk premium method is a more difficult way of estimating future rate of returns. In essence, this method attempts to calculate risk premiums for each asset class and then project them into the future. Jeremy Siegel, author of *Stocks for the Long Run,* has calculated that the risk premium for the stock market from 1802 through 1997 was approximately 7 percent. This premium of 7 percent added to the current one-year Treasury bill yield of about 1.5 percent results in an expected return for the overall stock market of 8.5 percent. This is well below the stock market's historical average return of about 10 percent. You can see that these two methods used for estimating future expected returns generate significantly different results.

The allocations in the table "Unconstrained Portfolio Optimization," on the previous page, were computed using expected returns, standard deviations, and correlations that were preloaded into the portfolio optimization software. Relying solely on pre-loaded inputs may be prudent, but it can lead to some unrealistic return expectations. I do not attempt to constrain

Default Portfolios

ASSET CLASS	INDEX	EXPECTED RETURN AFTER FEES
Short-Term Bonds	Lehman Bros. 1-3 year Gov't	3%
Intermediate-Term Bonds	Lehman Bros. Interm. Credit	4.5%
Large-Cap Stocks	S&P 500	7%
Small-Cap Stocks	Russell 2000	9%
International Stocks	MSCI EAFE (net)	7%
Real Estate Investment Trusts	Wilshire REIT	7.75%

Source: Hatton Consulting, Inc.

the software's expected standard deviations or correlations. I do, however, pay close attention to the pre-loaded expected return inputs. I have found at times that some of the expected returns for certain asset classes are not good estimates. For example, in the portfolio optimization software I use, the cash equivalent expected return is 3.25 percent (third quarter release 2004). Yet the current six-month Treasury bill—an appropriate benchmark for cash equivalents—is yielding 1.49 percent. In addition, this software estimates the annual expected return of large company growth stocks to be 10.75 percent, even though this is actually *greater* than the historical return of this asset class. These software inputs possibly overstate expected returns significantly, which can result in inappropriate asset allocations. An inappropriate asset allocation may negatively affect an investor's ability to reach his goals and objectives.

To avoid such problems, I have created eight well-diversified portfolios using six asset classes, shown in the table below. Throughout this book, I will refer to them as our "default" portfolios.

20/80	30/70	40/60	50/50	60/40	70/30	80/20	100/0
40	35	30	25	20	15	10	0
40	35	30	25	20	15	10	0
6	9	12	15	18	21	24	30
6	9	12	15	18	21	24	30
6	9	12	15	18	21	24	30
2	3	4	5	6	7	8	10

Default Portfolios—Expected and Range of Returns

PORTFOLIO	EXPECTED RETURN	1-YEAR RETURN RANGE %	3-YEAR AVG. RETURN RANGE %	5-YEAR AVG. RETURN RANGE %
20/80	4.5%	−4.8 to 15.8	−0.6 to 10.8	0.6 to 8.7
30/70	4.9%	−6.8 to 20.3	−1.5 to 12.7	−0.6 to 10.2
40/60	5.3%	−9.2 to 25.2	−2.7 to 15.5	−1.8 to 11.8
50/50	5.7%	−11.6 to 30.9	−3.9 to 18.1	−2.9 to 13.7
60/40	6.1%	−14.1 to 36.2	−6.6 to 24.3	−3.8 to 15.7
70/30	6.5%	−16.6 to 41.3	−6.1 to 22.2	−4.8 to 17.6
80/20	6.9%	−19.1 to 46.2	−7.2 to 24.7	−6.1 to 19.4
100/0	7.6%	−24.1 to 55.8	−10.4 to 29.4	−8.5 to 22.8

Note: The range of returns reflect two standard deviations.

Source: Hatton Consulting, Inc.

I then estimated the after-cost returns (projections done without accounting for expenses will overstate the expected return on the portfolio for the investor, potentially leading to a misaligned risk tolerance and creating a false sense of security) for each asset class and ran the constrained portfolios that resulted through my portfolio optimization software. The table above, "Default Portfolios—Expected and Range of Returns," displays the expected returns and ranges of returns for each such portfolio.

You may have noticed that the future estimated expected returns I have generated are less than the corresponding historical returns. How then do I determine if such returns are appropriate if they differ from the pre-loaded returns in the portfolio optimization software? William Bernstein, author of *The Intelligent Asset Allocator* and *The Four Pillars of Investing* (both books are highly recommended for investment advisers), describes a technique for estimating future returns. This tech-

Components of Stock Returns

RETURN FOR THE S&P 500	JAN. 1946– DEC. 1968	JAN. 1969– DEC. 1981	JAN. 1982– MAR. 2000
Initial Dividend Yield	5.0%	3.1%	5.8%
Growth in Earnings	6.6%	8.0%	6.8%
Expansion/Contraction of P/E	2.4%	–5.5%	5.7%
Average Annual Return	**14.0%**	**5.6%**	**18.3%**

Source: Adapted from a presentation by Professor Burton Malkiel

nique, espoused by John Bogle and Burton Malkiel (among others), uses the following formula:

Market return = Current dividend yield + earnings growth
+ expansion/contraction of P/E multiple

Bernstein notes that for the twentieth century, the average annual dividend yield of the stock market was about 4.5 percent while the compounded earnings growth rate was about 5.0 percent. Adding these two numbers produces a total return of 9.5 percent; nonetheless, the *actual* return for this period was 11.22 percent. The difference of 1.72 percentage points (11.22 percent versus 9.50 percent) can be attributed to the expansion of the P/E (price/earnings) multiple. The table above, "Components of Stock Returns," shows the results for different past time periods using the preceding formula.

The preceding formula changes when it is used to compute the future expected returns of bonds:

Market return = Current coupon (or yield to maturity) +/–
effect of increasing or decreasing interest rates

Components of Bond Returns

LEHMAN AGGREGATE BOND INDEX	JAN. 1946–DEC. 1968	JAN. 1969–DEC. 1981	JAN. 1982–MAR. 2000
Initial Interest Yield	2.7%	5.9%	13.0%
Effect of Increasing or Decreasing Rates	–0.9%	–2.9%	0.3%
Average Annual Return	**1.8%**	**3.8%**	**13.3%**

Source: Adapted from a presentation by Professor Burton Malkiel

The table above shows the historical results for bond returns, using this modified formula, for the same three time periods.

Are the techniques that I have just cited for estimating future expected returns any better than the historical or risk premium methods? While I feel confident that they are, that does not mean other techniques or methods are not prudent. Any of them are legally defensible if they are part of a rational *process* that is used to estimate future expected returns.

In an example earlier in this Practice, I determined a portfolio's target rate of return (TRR) to be 7 percent. To reiterate, the TRR is the return an investor's portfolio needs to earn to accomplish her goals and objectives. Once the TRR is determined, I speak with the investor about the potential negative returns associated with a portfolio designed to achieve any given TRR. This discussion is very critical because the investor needs to thoroughly understand the potential risks associated with the TRR that has been calculated for her portfolio and whether she is willing to accept those risks. I engage in the following discussion to help ensure a true understanding by the investor.

I first discuss the potential range of returns for a portfolio comprised of 80 percent stocks and 20 percent fixed-income investments—a portfolio with a TRR of 7 percent. In this portfolio, the downside risk is –19.1 percent, so if the investor has a $1 million portfolio, it could possibly decline in value by about $200,000. I am careful to *communicate the percentage decline in dollars.* I also point out to the investor that any loss is not permanent; assuming that the portfolio is well diversified, any significant decline in value should only be temporary.

I find it extremely helpful for the investor to see the actual annual returns, shown in the table on the following two pages, "Annual Returns for Default Portfolios," for the default portfolios that are associated with the various TRRs. Great value can come from this discussion because the investor typically relives his experience for particular years. I almost invariably find that investors have made the same mistakes time and again. They usually become more aggressive after good performing years and less aggressive after bad performing years—just the *opposite* of what they should have done. Investors tend to realize after this part of the discussion that there is usually *more, not less, risk* in the market after a strong period of positive performance.

Another important point that I cover with investors is the tendency for them to focus on annualized returns. When an investor focuses on an annualized return, he tends to assume that that return will be what he will get going forward on a year-by-year basis. I cannot stress how important it is to point out to an investor that annualized rates of return are very different from returns that happen year by year. This fact can have a significant impact on portfolios where investors need to take withdrawals. (I will cover this issue in just a moment.)

I also cover one more set of numbers with investors. This may seem like overkill to some, but it is one more step I may take

Annual Returns for Default Portfolios, 1973–2003

YEAR	20/80	30/70	40/60	50/50	60/40	70/30	80/20	100
1973	−1.0	−4.0	−6.9	−9.8	−12.7	−15.5	−18.2	−23.6
1974	−0.1	−3.5	−6.8	−10.1	−13.2	−16.3	−19.4	−25.2
1975	14.6	18.2	21.9	25.6	29.3	33.1	36.9	44.8
1976	12.1	13.9	15.6	17.4	19.2	20.9	22.7	26.2
1977	5.4	6.0	6.6	7.2	7.8	8.4	9.0	10.2
1978	7.5	9.0	10.5	11.9	13.4	14.8	16.3	19.2
1979	11.2	12.8	14.3	15.9	17.4	19.0	20.6	23.7
1980	13.9	16.2	18.5	20.7	22.9	25.2	27.4	31.8
1981	10.9	9.5	8.2	6.9	5.6	4.3	3.0	0.4
1982	18.8	18.4	18.0	17.6	17.2	16.8	16.3	15.3
1983	12.2	13.9	15.6	17.3	19.0	20.8	22.5	26.1
1984	11.1	10.2	9.4	8.5	7.6	6.7	5.8	4.0
1985	17.5	19.7	22.0	24.3	26.6	28.9	31.3	36.1
1986	13.5	15.4	17.2	19.1	20.9	22.8	24.7	28.6
1987	6.0	6.3	6.5	6.6	6.6	6.5	6.3	5.7
1988	9.9	11.5	13.1	14.8	16.4	18.0	19.7	23.1
1989	12.3	13.0	13.7	14.4	15.0	15.7	16.4	17.7
1990	3.6	1.1	−1.3	−3.8	−6.2	−8.6	−11.0	−15.7
1991	14.0	15.9	17.7	19.5	21.4	23.2	25.1	28.7

to help investors understand the potential of the market. The table on pages 92–93, "Best and Worst Twelve-Month Periods for Default Portfolios," shows rolling returns for one-, three-, five-, ten-, and twenty-year periods of time. For example, there are 361 one-year rolling periods: January 1, 1973 to January 1, 1974; February 1, 1973 to February 1, 1974; and so on. The worst calendar year for a one-year period for the 80/20 portfolio was –19.4 percent in 1974 (table above). Notice that the worst twelve-month period for the 80/20 portfolio was –31.1 percent, from October 1973 through September 1974—a more significant

YEAR	20/80	30/70	40/60	50/50	60/40	70/30	80/20	100
1992	5.5	5.5	5.5	5.5	5.5	5.5	5.4	5.4
1993	8.7	10.1	11.5	12.9	14.3	15.7	17.2	20.1
1994	1.3	1.5	1.7	1.8	2.0	2.1	2.2	2.5
1995	13.2	14.5	15.9	17.2	18.6	19.9	21.3	24.1
1996	7.1	8.4	9.6	10.9	12.2	13.5	14.7	17.3
1997	9.1	10.3	11.6	12.8	14.0	15.3	16.5	18.9
1998	8.1	8.6	9.2	9.7	10.1	10.5	10.9	11.4
1999	6.0	7.8	9.6	11.4	13.2	15.0	16.8	20.5
2000	5.6	4.3	3.0	1.8	0.5	−0.7	−2.0	−4.6
2001	3.7	2.3	0.8	−.6	−2.2	−3.7	−5.2	−8.3
2002	1.0	−1.2	−3.6	−5.9	−7.0	−10.4	−12.7	−17.1
2003	9.1	12.5	15.9	19.4	24.0	26.6	30.3	38.0
Annualized Return 79–03	**8.7**	**9.1**	**9.5**	**9.9**	**10.3**	**10.6**	**11.0**	**11.5**
Annualized Standard Deviation	**3.9**	**5.1**	**6.5**	**7.9**	**9.3**	**10.8**	**12.3**	**15.2**
Growth of $1	**$13.29**	**$15.08**	**$16.99**	**$19.01**	**$21.12**	**$23.29**	**$25.51**	**$29.92**

Source: DFA Returns Program

decline than the calendar year. As we move to the three-, five-, ten-, and twenty-year rolling periods, we gain additional insight into what the market has delivered. Investors appreciate this lesson in investment history; education can be a powerful tool in gaining an investor's trust and elevating their confidence in the decisions they make. The three factors of range of returns, annual returns, and rolling periods of returns allow an investor to more confidently identify their risk tolerance.

Investors that do not need to make portfolio withdrawals will benefit the most from the preceding discussion on identifying risk

Best and Worst Twelve-Month Periods for Default Portfolios

	STOCK/ BOND	STOCK/ BOND	STOCK/ BOND
1-Year Returns			
361 Periods	**20/80**	**30/70**	**40/60**
Best Return %	25.1 (Jul-82)	29.2 (Jul-82)	33.4 (Jul-82)
Worst Return %	−5.0 (Oct-73)	−9.8 (Oct-73)	−14.4 (Oct-73)
3-Year Returns			
337 Periods			
Best Return %	16.9 (Apr-84)	18.2 (Apr-84)	20.6 (Apr-84)
Worst Return %	2.7 (Apr-00)	0.7 (Apr-00)	−1.1 (Apr-00)
5-Year Returns			
313 Periods			
Best Return %	15.8 (Sep-81)	17.3 (Aug-82)	19.0 (Aug-82)
Worst Return %	4.1 (Apr-98)	3.2 (Apr-98)	2.3 (Apr-98)
10-Year Returns			
253 Periods			
Best Return %	12.8 (Nov-79)	13.9 (Sep-77)	15.1 (Sep-77)
Worst Return %	5.9 (Apr-93)	6.0 (Apr-93)	6.1 (Apr-93)
20-Year Returns			
133 Periods			
Best Return %	10.6 (Sep-74)	11.4 (Oct-74)	12.3 (Oct-74)
Worst Return %	8.1 (May-83)	8.5 (May-83)	8.8 (Apr-83)
Annualized Return	**8.7**	**9.1**	**9.5**
Growth of $1	**$13.29**	**$15.08**	**$16.99**

Source: DFA Returns Program

tolerance. However, investors that require monthly, quarterly, or yearly portfolio withdrawals need to understand the potential effects of the withdrawals. Why? The ending values of portfolios that have

STOCK/ BOND	STOCK/ BOND	STOCK/ BOND	STOCK/ BOND	STOCK/ BOND
50/50	**60/40**	**70/30**	**80/20**	**100/0**
37.8 (Jul-82)	42.2 (Jul-82)	46.8 (Jul-82)	51.5 (Jul-82)	61.2 (Jul-82)
−18.9 (Oct-73)	−23.1 (Oct-73)	−27.2 (Oct-73)	−31.1 (Oct-73)	−38.5 (Oct-73)
23.1 (Apr-84)	25.7 (Apr-84)	28.3 (Apr-84)	30.9 (Apr-84)	36.2 (Apr-84)
−3.0 (Apr-00)	−5.0 (Apr-00)	−6.9 (Apr-00)	−8.8 (Apr-00)	−12.6 (Apr-00)
21.0 (Aug-82)	23.0 (Aug-82)	25.0 (Aug-82)	27.1 (Aug-82)	31.2 (Aug-82)
1.4 (Apr-98)	0.4 (Apr-98)	−0.5 (Apr-98)	−1.5 (Apr-98)	−3.6 (Apr-98)
16.2 (Sep-77)	17.4 (Sep-77)	18.6 (Sep-77)	19.7 (Sep-77)	22.0 (Sep-77)
6.2 (Apr-93)	6.2 (Apr-93)	6.2 (Apr-93)	6.2 (Apr-93)	6.2 (Apr-93)
13.1 (Oct-74)	13.9 (Oct-74)	14.7 (Oct-74)	15.5 (Oct-74)	16.9 (Oct-74)
9.1 (Apr-83)	9.4 (Apr-83)	9.7 (Apr-83)	9.9 (Apr-83)	10.3 (Apr-83)
9.9	**10.3**	**10.6**	**11.0**	**11.5**
$19.01	**$21.12**	**$23.29**	**$25.51**	**$29.92**

the same beginning value, withdrawal rate, and *average* return can be significantly different as shown in the table on the following two pages, "Modeling Reality: The Monte Carlo Simulation."

Modeling Reality: The Monte Carlo Simulation

AGE	PORTFOLIO VALUE	RETURN	ANNUAL WITHDRAWAL	AGE	PORTFOLIO VALUE
65	$1,000,000			65	$1,000,000
66	$1,052,750	10.0%	$47,200	66	$1,064,000
67	$1,108,455	10.0%	$49,570	67	$1,064,319
68	$1,167,336	10.0%	$51,964	68	$1,087,202
69	$1,299,638	10.0%	$54,432	69	$1,252,808
70	$1,295,626	10.0%	$56,977	70	$1,243,085
71	$1,365,587	10.0%	$59,601	71	$1,436,539
72	$1,439,838	10.0%	$62,308	72	$1,788,160
73	$1,518,723	10.0%	$65,099	73	$2,067,729
74	$1,602,619	10.0%	$67,977	74	$2,234,453
75	$1,691,936	10.0%	$70,944	75	$2,387,809
76	$1,787,126	10.0%	$74,004	76	$2,576,287
77	$1,888,681	10.0%	$77,158	77	$2,734,891
78	$1,997,138	10.0%	$80,411	78	$2,930,428
79	$2,113,086	10.0%	$83,765	79	$2,830,953
80	$2,237,172	10.0%	$87,223	80	$3,021,816
81	$2,370,102	10.0%	$90,788	81	$3,141,960
82	$2,512,649	10.0%	$94,463	82	$3,526,775
83	$2,665,661	10.0%	$98,252	83	$3,180,766
84	$2,830,069	10.0%	$102,159	84	$3,548,674
85	$3,006,890	10.0%	$106,186	85	$3,789,220
86	$3,197,241	10.0%	$110,338	86	$4,158,711
87	$3,402,348	10.0%	$114,617	87	$4,838,404
88	**$3,623,554**	**10.0%**	**$119,029**	**88**	**$4,428,941**
89	$3,862,232	10.0%	$123,577	89	$4,824,978
90	$4,120,299	10.0%	$128,266	90	$4,863,306

Source: Hatton Consulting

RETURN	ANNUAL WITHDRAWAL	AGE	PORTFOLIO VALUE	RETURN	ANNUAL WITHDRAWAL
		65	$1,000,000		
11.1%	$47,200	**66**	$987,917	3.5%	$47,200
4.6%	$49,570	**67**	$982,942	4.5%	$49,570
7.0%	$51,964	**68**	$1,005,687	7.6%	$51,964
20.1%	$54,432	**69**	$1,142,431	19.0%	$54,432
3.8%	$56,977	**70**	$1,015,042	−6.1%	$56,977
20.3%	$59,601	**71**	$901,536	−5.3%	$59,601
28.8%	$62,308	**72**	$840,090	0.0%	$62,308
19.2%	$65,099	**73**	$954,783	21.4%	$65,099
11.3%	$67,977	**74**	$939,009	5.4%	$67,977
10.0%	$70,944	**75**	$831,282	−3.9%	$70,944
10.9%	$74,004	**76**	$867,871	13.3%	$74,004
9.1%	$77,158	**77**	$725,451	−7.5%	$77,158
10.0%	$80,411	**78**	$670,350	3.4%	$80,411
−0.5%	$83,765	**79**	$620,492	5.0%	$83,765
9.8%	$87,223	**80**	$502,584	−4.9%	$87,223
6.9%	$90,788	**81**	$467,845	11.1%	$90,788
15.2%	$94,463	**82**	$429,138	11.9%	$94,463
−7.0%	$98,252	**83**	$410,885	18.6%	$98,252
14.7%	$102,159	**84**	$340,719	7.7%	$102,159
9.7%	$106,186	**85**	$239,667	1.5%	$106,186
12.6%	$110,338	**86**	$164,377	14.6%	$110,338
19.1%	$114,617	**87**	$76,401	16.2%	$114,617
−6.0%	**$119,029**	**88**	**$0**	**1.6%**	**$119,029**
11.7%	$123,577	**89**	$0	7.1%	$123,577
3.4%	$128,266	**90**	$0	15.9%	$128,266

All three of the simulations in this table have a beginning balance of $1 million, an initial annual withdrawal of $47,200, an assumed inflation of 3 percent, an average return of 10 percent, and a standard deviation of 10 percent. Traditional planning software runs projections like the one in Simulation 1, which assume that the average return occurs each year; that is, a 10 percent return and a 0 percent standard deviation (i.e., no risk). If a portfolio contains investments that are not guaranteed to generate a particular return at a particular time (i.e., stocks), we know that the return will vary each year as in Simulations 2 and 3. Although an investor in each of the three simulations started with the same amount of money and withdrew the same inflation-adjusted income, you can see that the ending portfolio values at age eighty-eight are significantly different. An investor in Simulation 1 ends up with $3,682,232, in Simulation 2 ends up with $4,428,941, and in Simulation 3 ends up with $0!

Monte Carlo Simulation attempts to more accurately model the realities (including sometimes wildly gyrating values) of financial markets. Instead of running three static simulations, such as those shown in the table on the previous two pages, Monte Carlo Simulation software can run thousands of simulations in the effort to calculate a portfolio "success rate." If the goal of the investor in the Monte Carlo Simulation table was to receive inflation-adjusted income and retain her original $1 million (not inflation-adjusted) intact at age 88, then the simulation had a "success rate" of 66 percent (i.e., two of the three simulations projected a portfolio value greater than $1 million). I have been told by experts in Monte Carlo Simulation that a minimum success rate of 80 percent is adequate.

Monte Carlo Simulation is an excellent tool, in my opinion. However, like portfolio optimization software, the outputs it produces are highly sensitive to its inputs: garbage in, garbage out. While Monte Carlo software is a sophisticated tool, make sure that you understand all aspects, especially the sensitivity of the inputs, before you use it. Please note that this explanation of Monte Carlo Simulation is highly simplified and is meant only as an introduction to those of you that have not yet been exposed to it.

I have now identified a TRR needed to achieve the goals and objectives of an investor. I also have shown the possible future portfolio outcomes based on the default portfolios' current expected ranges of return and what has actually happened to such portfolios over different past time periods. If an investor is now willing to accept the volatility that is associated with their TRR, you can design a specific asset allocation for the investor (based on the broad split between growth and fixed-income investments). If the investor is not comfortable with the risk level of his portfolio, then they must adjust their goals and objectives so that they can invest in a portfolio that does comport with his particular level of risk. When this process is complete, we have identified the risk level of the investor's portfolio. *It is critical to repeat this process annually; it is rare for an initial asset allocation to remain suitable over the lifetime of an investor.*

Practice 2.2: *An expected modeled return to meet investment objectives has been identified.*

A modeled return is simply the expected rate of return and the probable range of returns that are associated with it. In the absence of a trust document defining the rate of return for the portfolio, actuarial reports for a defined benefit plan or a minimum spending policy for a foundation, the adviser needs to determine what rate of return will allow the investor to meet the goals and objectives of the portfolio.

An adviser that follows a prudent process to determine a portfolio's modeled return will not be held legally liable if the portfolio fails to earn its expected return. I showed you in Practice 2.1 that defining a portfolio's risk level, in effect, defines its modeled return. In that example, it was determined that a 7 percent modeled return would achieve the investor's goals and objectives. From the table on page 86 we can see the 80/20 portfolio offers the closest return to 7 percent. The actual modeled return is 6.9 percent with a range of returns of –19.1 percent to 46.2 percent for the one-year tolerable return range. The following excerpt is from an investment policy statement; it shows how I communicate the concept of a modeled return to investors.

> It has been determined that the stated overall asset allocation is expected to achieve a Modeled Return of 6.9%; this is the return necessary to achieve the stated goals and objectives. The Client understands this Target Rate of Return is a long term average and that there is a 95% probability of realizing a return that may range from a negative 19.1% to a positive 46.2% in any given year. Initial__________

It is very important to include this language in the investment policy statement. Even more important is the extra time I take to discuss carefully with investors the full implications of the language. After all, we all know with absolute certainty that there will always be times when financial markets negatively impact the value of investor portfolios. Investors should understand that earned returns *greater* than the expected return can also be seen as risky in the sense that positive returns are the mirror image of negative returns. I urge you to take the time to discuss this issue with investors and have them specifically acknowledge their understanding of it by initialing the investment policy statement (as noted). My experience has been that by doing so an investor is much calmer in down markets because they know *beforehand* that large and small dips in the value of her portfolio are bound to occur.

Practice 2.3: *An investment time horizon has been identified.*

One reason for the need to develop a five-year (or more) cash-flow analysis is to determine the investment time horizon of the investor. Here is how the Foundation for Fiduciary Studies defines a *time horizon:* "That point-in-time when more money is flowing out of the portfolio than is coming in from contributions and/or from portfolio growth. If the time horizon is less than five years, it is considered short, and if the time horizon is five years or more, it is considered long." This implies that a portfolio should be invested in fixed-income securities and cash if it needs to be liquidated within five years. If the portfolio's assets do not need to be liquidated within five years, the amount not needed within five years may be invested in stocks as well. Note that a time horizon is either long or short.

It is important to note that one investor can have multiple time horizons. A twenty-five-year-old saving money for a house that she wishes to purchase three to four years in the future, for example, should not invest her money in stocks because she has a short investment time horizon. The risk is that the value of the stocks could be depressed so much that there would not be enough time for the prices to recover within the desired time horizon. The same twenty-five-year old could have a long time horizon, though, when it comes to investing for her retirement. If she retires at sixty-five, for example, she has forty years to recover from any losses her portfolio has incurred by being invested in stocks. One implication of this is that investors with long time horizons have the option of investing in a greater number of asset classes. That's why it is important to tie an investor's time horizon to his or her specific goals.

Many investors and investment advisers believe that identifying the "best" money manager or mutual fund is the most impor-

The Hierarchy of Decisions

Most Important:	What is the time horizon of the investment strategy?
↓	What asset classes will be considered?
	What will be the mix among asset classes?
	What sub-asset classes will be considered?
Least Important:	Which managers/funds will be considered?

Source: Center for Fiduciary Studies

tant investment decision to be made. This widespread belief has been called into question by the Foundation for Fiduciary Studies. The Foundation has established what it calls the "Hierarchy of Decisions." This hierarchy of investment decision-making places the attempt to identify the best money manager or investment at the very bottom of the list because this decision is the *least important.* Identification of the investment time horizon is placed at the very top of the list because that decision is deemed to be the *most important.*

My own view coincides with that of the Foundation for Fiduciary Studies. That is, finding the best money manager or investment is the least important decision among those listed in priority by the Foundation.

Practice 2.4: *Selected asset classes are consistent with the identified risk, return, and time horizon.*

In the example in Practice 2.1, I identified a risk level derived from a maximum 80 percent stock, 20 percent bond portfolio allocation, and a modeled return associated with that risk level based on the default portfolios I created. One of the most challenging tasks for an adviser is to combine appropriate asset classes in a portfolio that will maximize return for a given level of risk. *It's important to note that there is no right or wrong answer for what asset classes should be used to construct a portfolio.*

The table on the following two pages, "Default Portfolios: Risk and Return," shows the default portfolios that I created, including the return and standard deviations for each portfolio. Each portfolio has six asset classes; I chose these combinations of asset classes because any investor can duplicate them with relative ease. I deviate from these portfolios when the time horizon or tax status of the investor is at issue. For example, if the time horizon is short (i.e., less than five years), I will not use any stock asset classes, and if the investor's account is not tax qualified, then I will consider including tax-free bonds in the portfolio.

And remember, use the fewest asset classes that will deliver the best portfolio risk/return ratio *after* taxes and costs.

Practice 2.5: *The number of asset classes is consistent with portfolio size.*

No formula exists for determining the right number and kind of asset classes that should be included in any given portfolio. The minimum number of asset classes is three for retirement plans that are subject to ERISA. Any ERISA-sanctioned retirement plan must provide a minimum of three investment options (including a stock fund, bond fund, and cash account) that span the full range of the risk/return ratio. ERISA is the only legislation that mandates, by amount and type, the minimum asset classes that must be represented in retirement plan trusts. The unique facts and circumstances of a particular investor will dictate the appropriate number and kind of investments in the investor's portfolio. Regardless of a portfolio's size, though, the goal is the same: maximize portfolio return for a given level of risk. It is

Default Portfolios: Risk and Return
Returns 1973–2003

ASSET CLASS	INDEX	20/80
Short-Term Bonds	90-day T-bills	40
Intermediate-Term Bonds	Lehman Intermediate Gov't/Credit	40
Large-Cap Stocks	S&P 500	6
Small-Cap Stocks	Russell 2000	6
International Stocks	MSCI EAFE (net)	6
Real Estate Investment Trusts	Wilshire REIT	2
Annualized Return, 1973–2003		**8.7%**
Annualized Standard Deviation		**3.9**

Source: DFA Returns Program

important to note that adding an asset class to a portfolio should be done solely because it improves the portfolio's risk/return ratio *after* fees and taxes. The following guidelines can help in determining the number of assets to include:

- ➢ Size of portfolio
- ➢ Investment expertise of decision makers
- ➢ Taxable versus nontaxable status
- ➢ Investment expenses; more asset classes may lead to more expense
- ➢ Legislative, investor, social, or trust restriction on asset classes
- ➢ Ability of decision makers to properly monitor chosen asset classes

The table on page 104, "Adding Asset Classes," lists the basic guidelines developed by the Foundation for Fiduciary Studies for adding asset classes to a portfolio.

30/70	40/60	50/50	60/40	70/30	80/20	100/0
35	30	25	20	15	10	0
35	30	25	20	15	10	0
9	12	15	18	21	24	30
9	12	15	18	21	24	30
9	12	15	18	21	24	30
3	4	5	6	7	8	10
9.1%	**9.5%**	**9.9%**	**10.3%**	**10.6%**	**11.0%**	**11.5%**
5.1	**6.5**	**7.9**	**9.3**	**10.8**	**12.3**	**15.2**

The following three tables—"Simple Asset Allocation for Portfolios of $20,000 and Less," "Simple Asset Allocation for Portfolios between $20,000 and $100,000," and "Asset Allocations for Portfolios of $100,000 and Greater"—show the three asset levels and corresponding asset allocations that I use in my own practice to construct portfolios. To reiterate, I have created the default portfolios because any investor, at very low cost, can invest in them with index funds. Another potential benefit is that the default portfolios are very efficient. These portfolios are starting points and can be modified depending on the unique facts and circumstances of each investor. Because cash needs vary according to the requirements of each investor, I have assumed for purposes of the following three tables that those needs have been met. All performance numbers and standard deviations in the table "Asset Allocation Risk/Reward Profile" (page 108) are for the period from 1973 through 2003.

Adding Asset Classes

NUMBER OF OPTIONS		ASSET CLASS
3		Large Blend, Multisector Fixed, Cash
4	Add	International Equity Blend
5	Add	Small Blend
6	Add	Intermediate Fixed
7	Add	Mid-Cap Blend
8	Add	Large Value, Large Growth
9	Add	Emerging Markets
10	Add	Real Estate
11	Add	High-Yield Bonds
12	Add	International Bond

Source: Center for Fiduciary Studies

As I have noted repeatedly, the sole reason to add an asset class to a portfolio is to improve the risk/return ratio. The table on page 108 shows, in general, that as asset classes are added, the portfolios risk/return profile improves.

I have found it difficult to improve the risk/return ratio of the twelve asset classes that comprise portfolios valued at

Simple Asset Allocation for Portfolios of $20,000 and Less

ASSET CLASS	INDEX	20/80
Large-Cap Stocks	S&P 500	20
Intermediate-Term Bonds	Lehman Int. Gov't/Credit	80

Source: Hatton Consulting, Inc.

$100,000 and more. I have not included any "alternative" asset classes such as commodities because my own experiences with these kinds of investments have always been less than what was promised. It is also very difficult to evaluate the performances of alternative investments. There is no question that no unified and complete database of information for alternative investments exists that could allow for objective analyses of their performances. In addition, academics have found these databases fraught with bias; that is, funds that cease to exist due to poor performance are not accounted for when calculating historical results. This has a tendency to inflate the average returns of these investments.

If you decide to venture into alternative investments, I recommend that you walk slowly and cautiously. *Most important*, do not fall into the trap of investing in alternative investments to bail you out in periods when stock or bond markets are experiencing difficulty, such as the stock market decline from 2000–2002. Investors turn to alternative investments during periods of uncertainty because their promoters promise that they will perform in a way "alternative," i.e., go up in value, to the way in which the market is performing, i.e., going down in value. Alternative investments thrive during such time of fear.

30/70	40/60	50/50	60/40	70/30	80/20	100/0
30	40	50	60	70	80	100
70	60	50	40	30	20	0

Simple Asset Allocation for Portfolios between $20,000 and $100,000

ASSET CLASS	INDEX	20/80
Short-Term Bonds	90-day T-bills	40
Intermediate-Term Bonds	Leh. Interm Gov't/Credit	40
Large-Cap Stocks	S&P 500	6
Small-Cap Stocks	Russell 2000	6
International Stocks	MSCI EAFE (net)	6
Real Estate Investment Trusts	Wilshire REIT	2

Source: Hatton Consulting, Inc.

Asset Allocations for Portfolios of $100,000 and Greater

ASSET CLASS	20/80
U.S. Stocks	
Large-Cap Stocks	3
Large Value Stocks	3
Small-Cap Stocks	3
Small Value Stocks	3
Real Estate Investment Trusts	2
International Stocks	
Large-Cap Stocks	3
Large Value Stocks	1
Small Value Stocks	1
Emerging Markets Stocks	1
Fixed Income	
Short-Term Fixed Income	40
Intermediate Fixed Income	40

Source: Hatton Consulting, Inc.

30/70	40/60	50/50	60/40	70/30	80/20	100/0
35	30	25	20	15	10	0
35	30	25	20	15	10	0
9	12	15	18	21	24	30
9	12	15	18	21	24	30
9	12	15	18	21	24	30
3	4	5	6	7	8	10

30/70	40/60	50/50	60/40	70/30	80/20	100/0
4.5	6	7.5	9	10.5	12	15
4.5	6	7.5	9	10.5	12	15
4.5	6	7.5	9	10.5	12	15
4.5	6	7.5	9	10.5	12	15
3	4	5	6	7	8	10
3	5	6	8	9	10	15
2	3	3	4	4	5	5
2	2	3	3	4	4.5	5
2	2	3	3	4	4.5	5
35	30	25	20	15	10	0
35	30	25	20	15	10	0

Asset Allocation Risk/Reward Profile

ALLOCATION	20/80	30/70	40/60	50/50	60/40	70/30	80/20	100/0
$20,000 and Less								
Annualized Return	9.2%	9.6%	9.9%	10.2%	10.4%	10.6%	10.8%	11.2%
Annualized Stan. Dev.	5.3	6.2	7.4	8.7	10.0	11.4	12.9	15.8
$20,000 to $100,000								
Annualized Return	8.7%	9.15	9.5%	9.9%	10.3%	10.6%	11.0%	11.5%
Annualized Stan. Dev.	3.9	5.1	6.5	7.9	9.3	10.8	12.3	15.2
$100,000 and Greater								
Annualized Return	9.1%	9.9%	10.5%	11.2%	11.7%	12.4%	13.0%	13.9%
Annualized Stan. Dev.	3.8	5.1	6.4	7.8	9.2	10.7	12.1	15.0

Source: DFA Returns Program

Be sure, then, to consider alternative investments only after you have conducted a thorough due diligence and believe they will improve investor chances of achieving their goals and objectives through an enhanced risk/return ratio.

Step Three

Formalize Investment Policy

Practices 3.1–3.7

A prudent fiduciary investment process has many small steps. Reducing the steps to writing enables all parties involved in the process of managing a portfolio to work from a common document, known as an investment policy statement (IPS), the preparation of which is arguably the most important function of the fiduciary and is the aim of Step Three. It is important to note that ERISA does not require the preparation of an IPS. However, it certainly is a best practice and an indication that fiduciaries are aware of their responsibilities. In addition, it is a document that the Department of Labor will request for an audit.

Practice 3.1: *There is detail to implement a specific investment strategy.*

The IPS promotes effective communication by virtue of a series of built-in checks and balances to ensure that all parties involved are living up to their responsibilities. This can be particularly valuable in times of stress, such as severe market downturns, where the validity of the assumptions that led to creation of the IPS is called into question.

The Foundation for Fiduciary Studies notes: "The Investment Policy Statement should have sufficient detail that a third party would be able to implement the investment strategy; be flexible enough that it can be implemented in a complex and dynamic financial environment and yet not be so detailed it requires constant revisions and updates." A well-written IPS is similar to a set of blueprints for a house. Any qualified contractor can build a house from a set of blueprints. An IPS should be like a set of blueprints from which any knowledgeable adviser can implement a portfolio's investment plan.

There are six elements that the Foundation recommends be covered in an IPS:

1) Purpose and background
2) Statement of objectives
3) Guidelines and investment policy
   a. Risk tolerance
   b. Time horizon
   c. Chosen asset classes
   d. Expected returns
4) Securities guidelines
5) Selection of money managers
6) Control procedures
   a. Define duties and responsibilities of all parties involved
   b. Define monitoring criteria for selected money managers
   c. Define criteria for performance reporting
   d. Define process for accounting for fees and expenses

An example of an Investment Policy Statement for a 401(k) retirement plan and one for a high-net-worth individual can be found in Appendix I.

The following Practices provide more detail for the six elements just listed.

Practice 3.2: *The investment policy statement defines the duties and responsibilities of all parties involved.*

There are many potential roles to be filled within the investment process; many of them differ depending on the type of account being managed. People involved in the investment process must have his or her role identified along with their duties. This is in accord with Practice 1.2 titled, "Fiduciaries are aware of their duties and responsibilities." The following list identifies the most important roles and duties of some of the primary entities involved in the investment process.

1) Investment Adviser/Consultant

a. Prepare and maintain investment policy statement
b. Provide sufficient asset classes with different risk/return profiles in order to maximize return for the given risk level
c. Prudently and objectively select investment options
d. Control and account for investment expenses
e. Monitor and supervise all service vendors and investment options

2) Investment Manager

As distinguished from the investment adviser/consultant who is responsible for managing the investment process, the investment manager is responsible for making investment decisions (e.g., security selection and price decisions). The specific duties and responsibilities of each investment manager are:

a. Manage the assets under their supervision in accordance with the guidelines and objectives outlined in their respective service agreements, prospectus, or trust agreement.

b. Exercise full investment discretion with regard to buying, managing, and selling assets held in the portfolios.

c. If managing a separate account (as opposed to a mutual fund or a commingled account), seek approval from the client prior to purchasing and/or implementing the following securities and transactions:

- ➢ Letter stock and other unregistered securities, commodities or other commodity contracts, and short sales or margin transactions;
- ➢ Securities lending and pledging or hypothecating securities;
- ➢ Investments in the equity securities of any company with a record of less than three years continuous operation, including the operation of any predecessor; and
- ➢ Investments for the purpose of exercising control of management.

d. Vote promptly all proxies and related actions in a manner consistent with the long-term interest and objectives of the portfolio as described in the IPS. Each investment manager shall keep detailed records of the voting of proxies and related actions and will comply with all applicable regulatory obligations.

e. Communicate to the client all significant changes pertaining to the fund it manages or the firm itself. Changes in ownership, organizational structure, financial condition, and professional staff are examples of changes to the firm in which the client is interested.

f. Effect all transactions for the portfolio subject "to best price and execution." If a manager utilizes brokerage from the portfolio assets to effect "soft dollar" transactions, detailed records will be kept and communicated to the client.

g. Use the same care, skill, prudence, and due diligence under the circumstances then prevailing that experienced investment professionals acting in a like capacity and fully familiar with such matters would use in like activities for like portfolios with like aims in accordance and compliance with all applicable laws, rules, and regulations.

h. If managing a separate account (as opposed to a mutual fund or a commingled account), acknowledge co-fiduciary responsibility by signing and returning a copy of the IPS.

3) Custodian

Custodians are responsible for the safekeeping of a portfolio's assets. The specific duties and responsibilities of a custodian include:

a. Maintain separate accounts by legal registration.

b. Value the holdings.

c. Collect all income and dividends owed to the portfolio.

d. Settle all transactions (buy-sell orders) initiated by the investment manager.

e. Provide monthly reports that detail transactions, cash flows, securities held and their current value, and change in value of each security and the overall portfolio since the previous report.

4) The Investor

If the investor is an individual or private trust, annually:

a. Provide investment adviser with an updated balance sheet highlighting all assets and liabilities. The information must be detailed enough for the investment adviser to determine the broad and sub-asset classes (including real estate holdings) in which the portfolio is currently invested.

b. Provide updates and estimates of all income sources and outflows for ensuing five-year period. Examples of income sources include Social Security payments, pensions, rents, and royalties. Examples of normal and extraordinary outflows include estimates of monthly living expenses (normal) and home improvement, new car, vacations (extraordinary).

c. Complete Practice 2.1 in order to determine maximum equity exposure and liquidity needs to reflect possible changes in the investor's circumstances.

d. Review long- and short-term goals and objectives.

e. Notify investment adviser of any material changes in the preceding circumstances subsequent to annual review.

5) Plan Sponsors and Investment Committee Members

Plan sponsors and investment committee members have the responsibility for ensuring that the following duties are carried out:

a. Determine investment goals and objectives.
b. Identify asset allocation policy.
c. Establish or approve (if prepared by the investment adviser/consultant) an explicit, written investment policy statement consistent with the written goals and objectives.
d. Approve appropriate money managers, mutual funds, or other "prudent experts" to implement the investment policy.
e. Avoid conflicts of interests and prohibited transactions.

It is important to note that plan sponsors and investment committee members are *required* under modern standards of prudent fiduciary investing to delegate the preceding duties to agents if they believe they do not possess the knowledge and skill to perform those duties. Plan sponsors and investment committee members should understand, though, that they *always retain* the overall duty to prudently select and monitor the prudent experts they hire.

Practice 3.3: *The investment policy statement defines diversification and rebalancing guidelines.*

The asset classes that have been selected for a portfolio as well as the amounts to be placed in each asset class should be documented in the IPS. The table at right, "Documenting the Asset Allocation," shows how this is done.

Documenting the Asset Allocation

ASSET CLASS	LOWER LIMIT %	TARGET ALLOCATION %	UPPER LIMIT %
Cash Equivalent	4.0	5	6.0
Large-Cap Stocks	7.5	10	12.5
Large Value Stocks	7.5	10	12.5
Small-Cap Stocks	7.5	10	12.5
Small Value Stocks	7.5	10	12.5
Real Estate (REITs)	4.0	5	6.0
Large-Cap International	7.5	10	12.5
Short-Term Bonds	15.0	20	25.0
Intermediate-Term Bonds	15.0	20	25.0

Source: Hatton Consulting, Inc.

The "Target Allocation %" in column three of the table is the percentage amount to be invested in each asset class. The "Lower Limit %" in column two and the "Upper Limit %" in column four represent the "trading range" within which an asset class will be allowed to fluctuate in value before a decision is made to buy or sell a portion of the asset class.

I recommend automatic rebalancing only for qualified, non-taxable accounts such as 401(k) plans because there are no tax ramifications; this recommendation does not hold, however, if there are high transaction costs associated with a rebalancing. For nonqualified, taxable accounts, I do not recommend automatic rebalancing because of the potential tax consequences of selling assets at a gain. Before making taxable sells to bring the portfolio back into balance, a few things can be considered. Either new cash from the investor or income from dividends and interest payments can be used to purchase additional shares of the under-represented asset classes. If these sources are insufficient to bring the portfolio back into balance, selling portions of the over-represented asset classes should be considered only after the tax consequences of any contemplated transaction are understood.

There are a number of benefits to having diversification and rebalancing guidelines spelled out in an IPS. This is important, since *the primary reason to rebalance is to maintain a portfolio's desired risk level.* The greatest benefit of the guidelines is that they create discipline and force an investor to make investment decisions in his best interests and avoid letting emotions govern his decisions. For example, many investors make the classic investment mistake of chasing performance. The period of the late 1990s is an example of this. From 1995 to 1999, large company growth stocks far exceeded their historical average returns. Over the same period, the return of small company value stocks was virtually zero. In the absence of well-disciplined diversification and rebalancing guidelines, many investors loaded up on their large company growth stock positions at the expense of small company value stocks.

As we now know, the fortunes of these asset classes reversed and many investors that had chased the performance of large company growth stocks suffered significant losses when small company value stocks outperformed. This lack of disciplined rebalancing led to increased volatility and decreased returns for many portfolios. It is important to understand that rebalancing redeems what may seem to be poor investment decisions. As long as an investor follows the diversification and rebalancing guidelines spelled out in the IPS, she or he will be forced to "buy low and sell high."

Where do you set the upper and lower limits of the trading range? There is no right or wrong answer, only guidelines. I recommend setting the limits 25 percent above and below the target asset allocation. This allows the value of an asset class to fluctuate freely enough to avoid unnecessary buying and selling in the portfolio. The following language, which is contained in an IPS prepared by Hatton Consulting, Inc., is a good example of the appropriate way in which to communicate rebalancing guidelines.

> ***Rebalancing of strategic allocation***—The adviser will consider rebalancing the portfolio back to the target allocation when the overall allocation or sub-asset classes deviate by plus or minus 25 percent. For example, if a particular asset class has a target allocation of 10 percent, rebalancing will be considered if that asset class falls to 7.5 percent or rises to 12.5 percent.
>
> ***Rebalancing is not automatic if an asset class reaches an upper or lower limit.*** Cash inflows/outflows will be deployed in such a way as to bring the portfolio back to the Target Allocation. *In the absence of inflows/outflows, transactions may be made only after all ramifications have been considered such as tax effects.*

Rebalancing also creates effective and positive communication between an investor and the investor's adviser. Investors want their money managed in a proactive manner; they appreciate knowing when and why transactions will take place *before* they actually take place. Rebalancing guidelines accomplish this.

Practice 3.4: *The investment policy statement defines due diligence criteria for selecting investment options.*

Defining how investment options will be selected is one of the most important functions of the IPS. The selection process must be defined in the IPS so that it can be carried out independently and objectively. Some of the greatest abuses in the recent mutual fund scandals arose from pay-to-play schemes. These occur when a mutual fund company pays (usually undisclosed) fees to a brokerage firm to induce the firm to recommend and sell the company's mutual funds. For example, an article in *The Wall Street Journal* estimated that Putnam Funds paid about $100 million a year to Edward D. Jones & Co. (a brokerage firm) to have Jones favor Putnam's mutual funds in the firm's sales offices.[1] This isn't illegal when it is fully disclosed (which rarely is adequately done), but it does create a conflict of interest that can call into question the independence and objectivity of a selection process. Another article from *The Wall Street Journal* reported that at the end of 2003, Morgan Stanley paid a fine of $50 million for what the SEC charged was "a company-wide failure to tell clients that it paid its brokers more to sell certain mutual funds that were more profitable to the firm." These are two examples of the ingrained behavior at some mutual fund companies and brokerage firms that help corrupt the process for selecting investment options. Such behavior is decidedly not in investors' best interests.

To counter this, I recommend that investment options be selected from open architecture trading platforms. The term *open architecture* simply means that an adviser has the ability to choose from a much wider variety of investment options that a "closed system" of, say, proprietary mutual funds. Fiduciary Analytics has created selection criteria for investment options, which I use in my own advisory practice. Fiduciary Analytics had three objectives in developing the criteria: (1) the process must be applicable to mutual funds and separate account managers; (2) it can be applied to any data base; and (3) it can be used for the both the searching and monitoring on the investment options.

Standardizing a due-diligence process for selecting the investment options in a portfolio is difficult because there are many different databases, such as Morningstar and Lipper. For example, a due-diligence process relies heavily on peer group/asset class comparisons. One database, though, may classify a certain investment option as a small value fund while another classifies it as a mid value fund. This is an example of why no process is perfect.

It is important to note that should an investment option not meet one or more of the selection criteria, it does not necessarily mean the option is somehow "bad" or should not be considered for inclusion in a portfolio. It simply means further investigation should be undertaken to understand why the option did not meet the selection criteria.

In my own practice, I have adopted the due-diligence process created by Fiduciary Analytics. There are eight screens of data: performance, risk-adjusted performance, minimum track record, correlation to peer group, minimum assets under management, style consistency, expenses/fees, and stability of organization. The following outlines the due diligence process that I use.

1) Performance relative to a peer group—The product's performance should be above the peer group's median manager return for one-, three-, and five-year cumulative periods.

2) Performance relative to assumed risk—The product's risk-adjusted performance (alpha and/or Sharpe ratio) should be above the peer group's median manager risk-adjusted performance for the latest three-year period.

3) Minimum track record—At least three years should have elapsed since the product's inception date.

4) Correlation to style or peer group—The product should be highly correlated to the asset class of the investment option. Within the Morningstar database, the category and style box should match.

5) Assets under management—The product should have at least $75 million under management.

6) Holdings consistent with style—The screened product should have no more than 20 percent of the portfolio invested in "unrelated" asset class securities. For example, a Large-Cap

Growth product should not hold more than 20 percent in cash, fixed-income, and/or international securities.
7) Expense ratios/fees—The product's fees should not be in the bottom quartile (i.e., most expensive 25 percent) of their peer group.
8) Stability of the organization—There should be no perceived organizational problems. The same portfolio management team should be in place for at least two years.

In addition to the preceding selection criteria for the due-diligence process, it is absolutely necessary to conduct some qualitative analysis. This includes knowing the philosophy of the fund company, the identity of the owners, the kinds of investors they serve and so forth. I will provide more detail about the qualitative aspects of the due-diligence process as well as actual results in Practices 4.1 through 4.4.

Practice 3.5: *The investment policy statement defines monitoring criteria for investment options and service vendors.*

Monitoring criteria for investment managers should be done utilizing the due-diligence process used for selecting investment options. At a minimum, quarterly reviews should be conducted to determine if the selected managers are performing adequately and adhering to the mandates of the relevant mutual fund prospectus or stated investment objectives for separately managed accounts. Fiduciary Analytics has developed a tool to help in this function called the Fiduciary Score. The Fiduciary Score aids in monitoring selected mutual funds on a quarterly basis and uses the eight selection criteria defined in Practice 3.4. The Foundation for Fiduciary Studies notes that "the Fiduciary Score provides an investment decision-maker with a flash report on a selected mutual fund or separate account manager. *It represents a suggested course of action and is not intended, nor should it be used, as the sole source of information for reaching an investment decision.*"

In the Fiduciary Score system, a mutual fund receives more points if it does not pass one or more of the eight selection criteria; if the fund passes all eight criteria, it receives a Fiduciary Score of 0. The following summarizes the potential range of actions a fiduciary can take if a mutual fund does not meet one or more of the criteria.

Passed—Fiduciary Score 0. No fiduciary due diligence shortfalls.

Appropriate—Fiduciary Score 1–25. The fund may be an appropriate choice for use in a fiduciary account.

Watch (2)—Fiduciary Score 26–50. The fund has noteworthy shortfalls. It may not be an appropriate choice if being considered in a search. However, if already in use, the fund may not need to be replaced.

Watch (3)—Fiduciary Score 51–75. The fund has considerable shortfalls. It may not be an appropriate choice if being considered in a search. However, if already in use, the fund may not need to be replaced.

Watch (4)—Fiduciary Score 76–100. The fund has significant shortfalls and may not be appropriate for use in a fiduciary account. Strongly consider replacing the fund if already in use.

The following four figures show the Fiduciary Score sheet results for four mutual funds, within the Large Blend peer group, when subjected to the selection criteria of the screening process. In the upper left corner you can see the fiduciary score for the latest quarter (data for quarter ended June 30, 2004) and the three-year average score. For the three funds that have shortfalls, the score sheet highlights with a gray box

Monitoring Investment Options

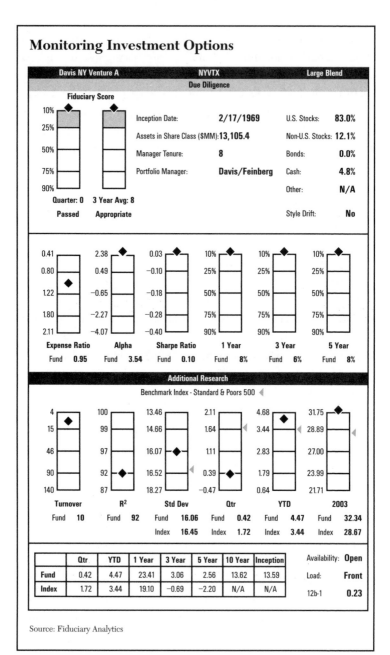

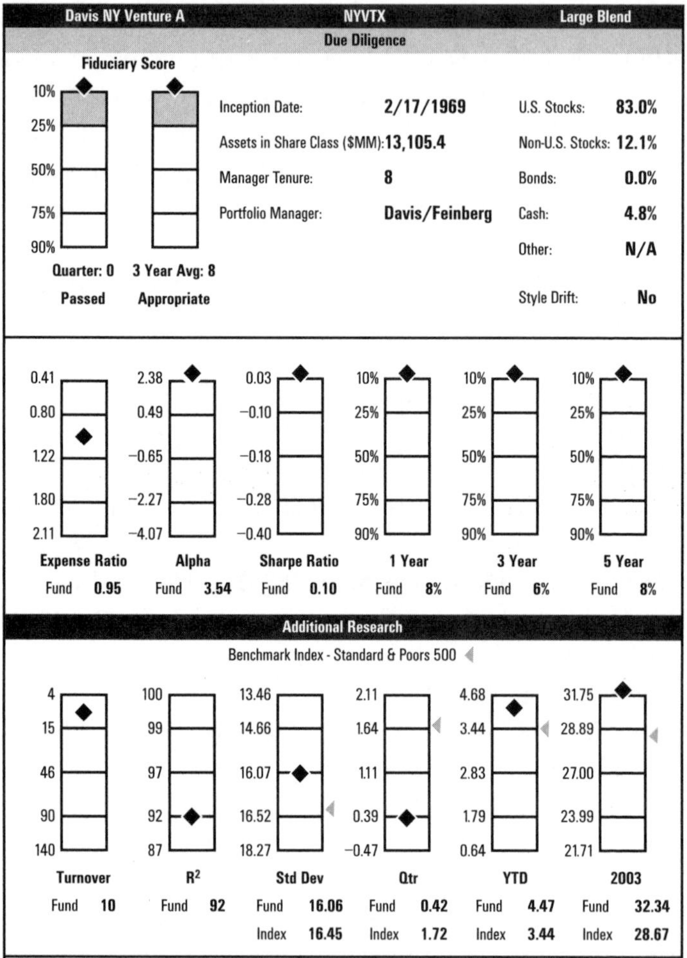

	Qtr	YTD	1 Year	3 Year	5 Year	10 Year	Inception
Fund	0.42	4.47	23.41	3.06	2.56	13.62	13.59
Index	1.72	3.44	19.10	−0.69	−2.20	N/A	N/A

Availability: **Open**

Load: **Front**

12b-1 **0.23**

Source: Fiduciary Analytics

Monitoring Investment Options

Dreyfus LifeTm Grth R | **DLGRX** | **Large Blend**

Due Diligence

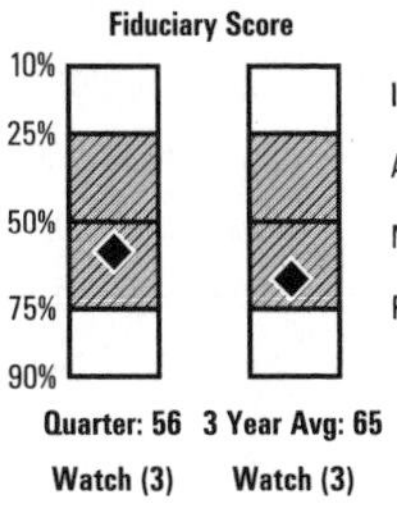

Inception Date: **3/31/1995**

Assets in Share Class ($MM) **75.8**

Manager Tenure: **0**

Portfolio Manager: **Reed, Jocelin A.**

U.S. Stocks: **58.7%**

Non-U.S. Stocks: **1.3%**

Bonds: **0.0%**

Cash: **39.7%**

Other: **N/A**

Style Drift: **No**

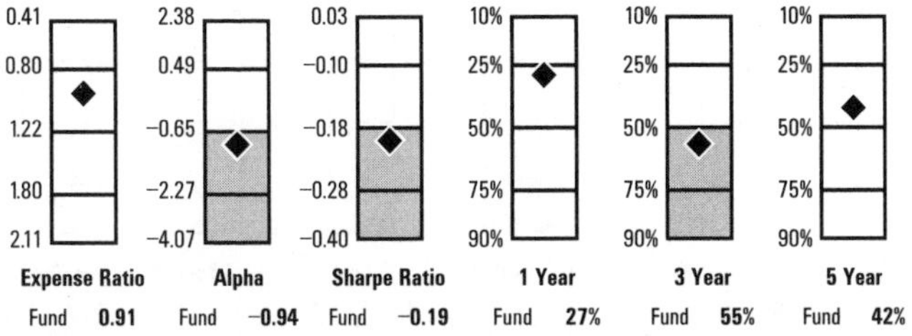

Additional Research

Benchmark Index - Standard & Poors 500

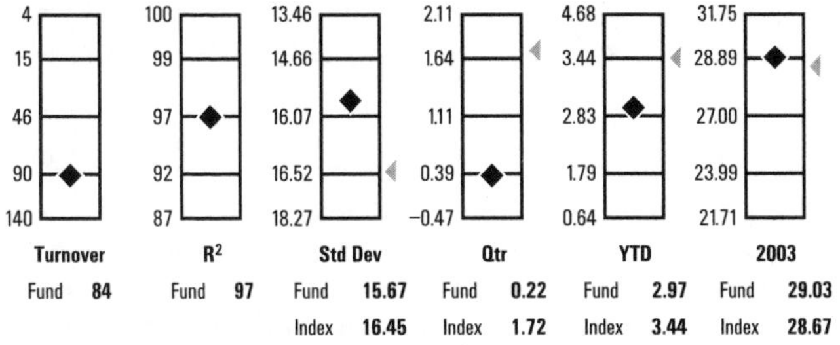

	Qtr	YTD	1 Year	3 Year	5 Year	10 Year	Inception
Fund	0.22	2.97	19.03	−1.48	−1.79	N/A	9.41
Index	1.72	3.44	19.10	−0.69	−2.20	N/A	N/A

Availability: **Open**

Load: **No**

12b-1 **0.00**

Source: Fiduciary Analytics

Monitoring Investment Options

Strong Gr & Inc Inv | **SGRIX** | **Large Blend**

Due Diligence

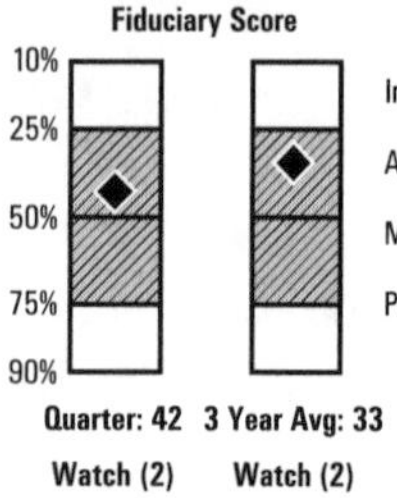

Inception Date: **12/29/1995**

Assets in Share Class ($MM): **520.8**

Manager Tenure: **8**

Portfolio Manager: **Milaitis, Rimas M.**

U.S. Stocks: **98.1%**

Non-U.S. Stocks: **1.6%**

Bonds: **0.0%**

Cash: **0.2%**

Other: **N/A**

Style Drift: **No**

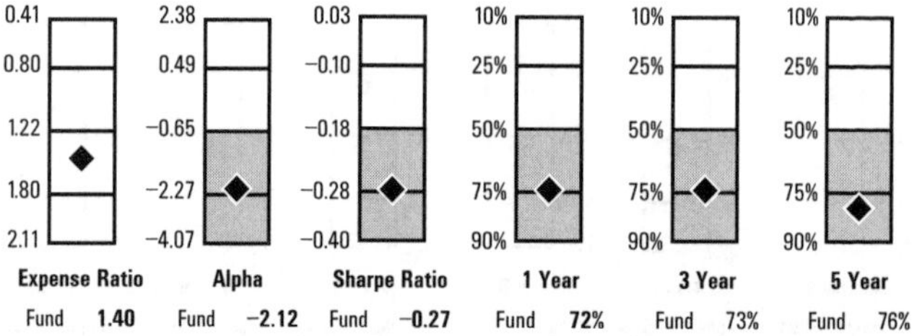

Additional Research

Benchmark Index - Standard & Poors 500

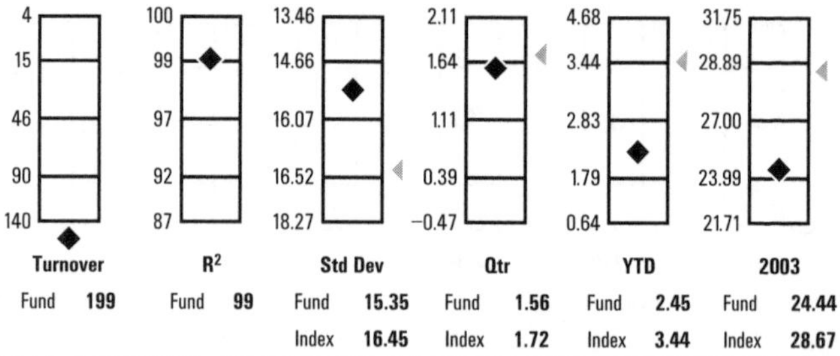

	Qtr	YTD	1 Year	3 Year	5 Year	10 Year	Inception
Fund	1.56	2.45	16.02	−2.63	−3.51	N/A	9.49
Index	1.72	3.44	19.10	−0.69	−2.20	N/A	N/A

Availability: **Open**

Load: **No**

12b-1 **0.00**

Source: Fiduciary Analytics

Monitoring Investment Options

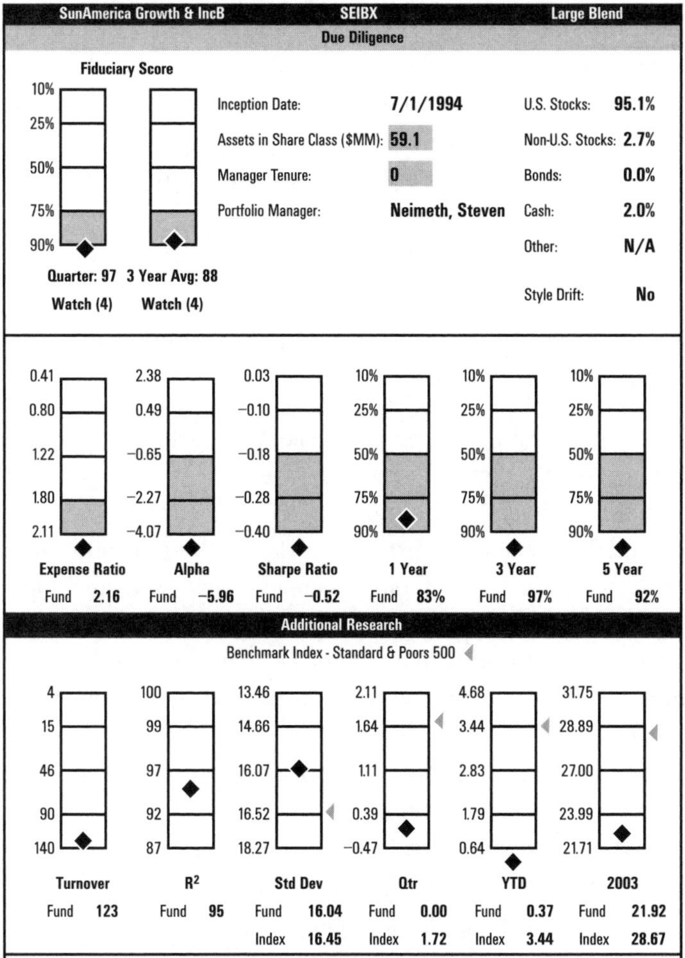

	Qtr	YTD	1 Year	3 Year	5 Year	10 Year	Inception
Fund	0.00	0.37	14.12	−6.71	−5.89	8.48	8.48
Index	1.72	3.44	19.10	−0.69	−2.20	N/A	N/A

Availability: **Open**
Load: **Deferred**
12b-1 **1.00**

Source: Fiduciary Analytics

the specific screening criteria that failed. For example, the Strong Growth and Income fund was below median for its alpha, Sharpe ratio, one-, three-, and five-year performance measurements.

These illustrations are excellent examples of how technology can be used to help fulfill fiduciary responsibility. They are concise, yet provide enough detailed information to ensure proper monitoring of mutual funds is conducted.

Practice 3.6: *The investment policy statement defines procedures for controlling and accounting for investment expenses.*

There are few things more complicated than the compensation structure erected by many firms in the professional investment business. A primary duty of fiduciaries is to incur only "appropriate" and "reasonable" investment costs for the portfolios under their care. Fiduciaries, though, cannot know what an "appropriate" or "reasonable" cost is unless it can first be identified. And investment costs often cannot be identified until they are "unbundled" (i.e., separated out). Investment management costs can be separated into four categories:

1) Money management fee for separate accounts or the annual expenses for mutual funds
2) Trading/custodial costs, including commissions
3) Broker/adviser/consulting fees and/or commissions
4) Administrative fees (for pension plans)

To control and account for all fees, I find it very helpful to create a table identifying the above fees and express the total as a percentage. The following example in the table at right, "Breakdown of Investment Costs," is a cost breakdown I provided a plan sponsor for a $2 million 401(k) plan.

Breakdown of Investment Costs

TYPE OF FEE	AMOUNT OF FEE
Annual Money Management Fee	117 basis points
Trading/Custodial	23 basis points
Adviser Fee	75 basis points
Administrative Fee	29 basis points
Total Fees	244 basis points

Note: 1% = 100 basis points.

Source: Hatton Consulting, Inc.

At least annually, the fees actually charged to the plan should be checked against what was written in the IPS and service agreements. Any differences should be investigated. Full disclosure of all fees is critical to fiduciary investing. In addition, full disclosure helps to foster trust and confidence between advisers and clients.

Practice 3.7: *The investment policy statement defines appropriately structured, socially responsible investment strategies (when applicable).*

Some investors want to incorporate social, ethical, moral, and/or religious criteria into their investment strategies. Their strong beliefs against, for example, tobacco, alcohol, and firearms lead them to exclude any stocks from their portfolios that are associated with companies manufacturing such products. This investment approach is referred to as socially responsible investing (SRI) (or mission-based investing).

Fiduciaries must be careful when dealing with any socially responsible investment strategy. Their duty is to ensure that any socially responsible strategy *does not* compromise portfolio perfor-

mance. However, a socially responsible investment can be deemed prudent if it passes an objective screening process. As a result, the investment may be considered for inclusion in a portfolio. There are three exceptions to this rule that fiduciaries governed by the standards of the Uniform Prudent Investor Act may allow:
1) The trust document for a private trust, foundation, or endowment must explicitly state the use of SRI strategy is appropriate;
2) A donor directs the use of a SRI strategy; or
3) A reasonable person would deduce from the mission statement of the foundation or endowment that SRI would be permitted. An example of this would be an alcohol treatment center that excludes the stocks of alcohol-producing companies from its endowment portfolio.

A fiduciary responsible for overseeing the selection and monitoring of investment options in a defined contribution plan such as a 401(k) plan is prudent when they offer a socially responsible fund that has been objectively screened. Screening for SRI strategies may include "qualitative" and "exclusionary" screens.

QUALITATIVE	**EXCLUSIONARY**
Community/consumer/employee relations	Product (alcohol, tobacco, firearms)
Environmental performance	Nuclear power, military weapons
Diversity	Life ethics

Language in an IPS should be explicit about the criteria for qualitative and exclusionary screens. For example, the stocks of companies that have poor employee relations, demonstrate lack of concern for the environment, practice racial or gender inequality, manufacture military weaponry, alcohol, tobacco, and firearm products, or operate nuclear facilities can all be excluded from investment portfolios. It is important to reiterate, though, that the IPS must be explicit about the kinds of company stocks that are to be excluded.

THE DOMINI 400 SOCIAL INDEX was created for a number of reasons, including the desire to gauge whether socially responsible investing would lead to inferior investment returns, the wish to create a benchmark for socially responsible investing, and the general need to define the meaning of socially responsible investing. The Domini 400 Social Index is comprised of 400 companies that are run through a number of exclusionary and qualitative screens. I recommend that the evaluation of any SRI strategy include measuring it against the Domini 400. For the ten-year period ending June 30, 2004 the Domini Social Equity fund returned 11.4 percent, compared to 11.8 percent for the S&P 500.

Step Four

Implement Policy

Practices 4.1–4.4

Fiduciaries are well advised to use professionals to implement all (or any part) of the investment management process described in this book when they feel they lack the necessary knowledge or skills to establish or implement this process on their own. Fiduciaries of ERISA retirement plans such as 401(k) plans must be particularly sensitive to this requirement since the law of ERISA holds them to a "prudent expert" standard. ERISA includes in its Prudent Man Rule the phrase "one familiar with such matters." This essentially requires fiduciaries to retain professionals with proven track records. After all, the primary role of a fiduciary is to manage the overall investment management process, not make specific investment decisions. Such decisions, along with others, should be delegated to experienced professionals who can prove by verifiable evidence that they have lived up to a high professional standard.

Practice 4.1: *The investment strategy is implemented in compliance with the required level of prudence.*

One of the most important functions of a fiduciary is to delegate to appropriate money managers. It is important that fiduciaries (and all other investors) understand the two fundamentally different approaches to investing: "active" investing and "passive" investing.

Those that believe in active investing employ specific security selection and market-timing techniques in attempts to "beat" the market return, and consider all (or at least most) financial markets as "inefficient." As noted in the discussion about Eugene Fama's Efficient Market Theory in Chapter 1, we know active investors believe that there are opportunities to identify stocks that are selling above or below their intrinsic value. In addition, we know they believe that stocks do not move in a "random walk" manner. Active investors also believe that it is possible to predict short-term increases or decreases in the values of specific stocks—or even the entire stock market. Active investment strategies are by far the dominant investment approach today.

Passive investors, on the other hand, believe that financial markets are "efficient" and that stocks move in a "random walk" manner. Instead of spending valuable time and money on an approach that they do not believe is worth the performance it generates (i.e., active investment strategies), passive investors buy index funds and asset class funds. These funds are generally more cost and tax efficient than actively managed mutual funds. They are invested in all the stocks that comprise a particular market benchmark such as the S&P 500 index or an asset class such as small company value stocks.

I have witnessed many heated arguments between proponents of active investing and passive investing. Although the active versus passive debate is a very divisive one, it need not extend to the world of prudent fiduciary investing, since both investment approaches are deemed to be prudent. Fiduciaries should, however, be aware of and understand the implications of both approaches to investing in order to defend the prudence of whichever approach they choose to follow. Reporter's General Note on Restatement Section 227 makes clear that proponents of active investing bear a greater burden of proof to justify their investment approach: "The greater the trustee's departure from one of the valid passive strategies, the greater is likely to be the burden of justification and also of continuous monitoring."[1]

In Practice 3.4, I outlined the due-diligence process for selecting and monitoring investment options. This process was established by Fiduciary Analytics, which also created a number of helpful tools that fiduciaries, particularly those following active investment strategies, can use to justify the decisions they make and actions they take. A good due-diligence process is characterized by the fact that it can be used for both mutual funds and separate account managers, it can be applied to any database, used for both selection and monitoring criteria, and can be applied to active and passive funds.

Most investors tend to focus heavily on past performance to help them select their investment options. This is a mistake for a number of reasons. The most critical is that consistent long-term performance is difficult to maintain. For example, for the period from 2001 through 2003, there were 4,780 funds in the large, mid, and small blend stock asset classes in the Morningstar database. Only 135 funds were able to achieve top-quartile performance for the entire three-year period, which is less than 3 percent of the total number of funds. Furthermore, for the five-year period of 1999 through 2003, there were 3,306 funds invested in the same three asset classes and only thirteen achieved top-quartile performance, which is about 0.4 percent of the total number of funds. In addition, I cited a study in Chapter 1 (see Appendix II) that illustrates how top-performing mutual funds for a five-year period were unable to repeat their superior performance in subsequent time periods. The simple yet profound lesson to be learned from this data is that *you must look beyond performance alone.*

To reiterate, the due-diligence process has eight criteria:

1) Performance relative to a peer group—The product's performance should be above the peer group's median manager return for one-, three-, and five-year cumulative periods.

2) Performance relative to assumed risk—The product's risk-adjusted performance (alpha and/or Sharpe ratio) should be above the peer group's median manager's risk-adjusted performance for the latest three-year period.

3) Minimum track record—At least three years should have elapsed since the product's inception date.

4) Correlation to style or peer group—The product should be highly correlated to the asset class of the investment option. Within the Morningstar database, the category and style box should match.

5) Assets under management—The product should have at least $75 million under management.

6) Holdings consistent with style—The screened product should have no more than 20 percent of the portfolio invested in "unrelated" asset class securities. For example, a Large-Cap Growth product should not hold more than 20 percent in cash, fixed income and/or international securities.

7) Expense ratios/fees—The product's fees should not be in the bottom quartile (i.e., the most expensive 25 percent) of their peer group.

8) Stability of the organization—There should be no perceived organizational problems—the same portfolio management team should be in place for at least two years.

The figure on pages 136–137, "Investment Option Screening Results," applies the eight criteria of the due-diligence process established by Fiduciary Analytics. It shows that of 15,485 funds in the Morningstar database at the end of March 2004, only 1,029 funds (or less than 7 percent of the total number) passed all eight selection criteria.

Of the 1,445 Large Blend funds in the database for this quarter ninety-six of them passed. Interestingly, of those ninety-six I counted forty-five that were index funds. I do not mean for this to be a treatise on active or passive mutual funds; rather, my aim is to show how to analyze both active and passive funds from an objective viewpoint. Screening all funds on the basis of the eight selection criteria—not whether they utilize an active or passive strategy—is very useful in determining the merits of either strategy.

It's important to remember that the purpose of this process is not to aid in making hard and fast decisions or to change the minds of those devoted to active or passive strategies. Rather, the process should be used to screen for investments that may merit inclusion in portfolios. What is also important to remember is that the process is a rational and well-defined one that can be justified as meeting the standard for prudent implementation. It is also important to know that this selection process is a best practice; it is not required by law.

Practice 4.2: *The fiduciary is following applicable "safe harbor" provisions (when elected).*

"Safe harbor" rules are created by the government to allow fiduciaries that elect to comply with them the opportunity to reduce their potential liability for investing and managing portfolio assets. There are two kinds of safe harbor rules: those that pertain to investment decisions made by *investment committees or investment advisers,* and those that pertain to investment decisions made by *participants in a retirement plan* such as a 401(k) plan.

Investment Option Screening Results

	Q1 2004–03/31/2004		
PEER GROUPS	TOTAL FUNDS	PASSED FUNDS	PASSING RATE
Bank Loan	44	5	11.36%
Bear Market	42	2	4.76%
Conservative Allocation	312	23	7.37%
Convertibles	69	4	5.80%
Diversified Emerging Mkts	168	14	8.33%
Diversified Pacific/Asia	33	3	9.09%
Emerging Markets Bond	49	1	2.04%
Europe Stock	143	6	4.20%
Foreign Large Blend	465	38	8.17%
Foreign Large Growth	206	15	7.28%
Foreign Large Value	136	11	8.09%
Foreign Small/Mid-Growth	93	8	8.60%
Foreign Small/Mid-Value	41	4	9.76%
High-Yield Bond	431	34	7.89%
High-Yield Muni	79	12	15.19%
Intermediate Government	361	11	3.05%
Intermediate-Term Bond	900	53	5.89%
Japan Stock	48	1	2.08%
Large Blend	1445	96	6.64%
Large Growth	1253	78	6.23%
Large Value	998	61	6.11%
Latin America Stock	22	2	9.09%
Long Government	42	1	2.38%
Long-Term Bond	70	3	4.29%
Mid-Cap Blend	354	16	4.52%
Mid-Cap Growth	787	39	4.96%
Mid-Cap Value	307	9	2.93%
Moderate Allocation	929	89	9.58%
Multisector Bond	170	18	10.59%
Muni California Int/Sh	60	3	5.00%
Muni California Long	138	2	1.45%
Muni Florida	90	10	11.11%

(continued)

PEER GROUPS	Q1 2004–03/31/2004 TOTAL FUNDS	PASSED FUNDS	PASSING RATE
Muni Massachusetts	63	6	9.52%
Muni Minnesota	50	6	12.00%
Muni National Interm	234	18	7.69%
Muni National Long	263	19	7.22%
Muni National Short	105	11	10.48%
Muni New Jersey	65	7	10.77%
Muni New York Int/Sh	64	6	9.38%
Muni New York Long	87	1	1.15%
Muni Ohio	53	9	16.98%
Muni Pennsylvania	80	8	10.00%
Muni Single State Int/Sh	276	24	8.70%
Muni Single State Long	266	5	1.88%
Pacific/Asia ex-Japan Stk	81	5	6.17%
Short Government	162	14	8.64%
Short-Term Bond	319	21	6.58%
Small Blend	388	17	4.38%
Small Growth	674	46	6.82%
Small Value	278	12	4.32%
Specialty-Communications	39	1	2.56%
Specialty-Financial	108	5	4.63%
Specialty-Health	193	9	4.66%
Specialty-Natural Res	92	4	4.35%
Specialty-Precious Metals	44	3	6.82%
Specialty-Real Estate	185	6	3.24%
Specialty-Technology	300	14	4.67%
Specialty-Utilities	75	5	6.67%
Ultrashort Bond	102	16	15.69%
World Allocation	63	4	6.35%
World Bond	132	14	10.61%
World Stock	359	41	11.42%
Totals	**15485**	**1029**	**6.65%**

Source: Fiduciary Analytics

The ERISA safe harbor rules establish five criteria pertaining to situations where investment decisions are made by an investment committee or investment adviser:

1) Use prudent experts to make investment decisions. Prudent experts are professional money managers such as banks, insurance companies, registered investment advisers, mutual funds, and separate account managers. If a fiduciary chooses to make investment decisions on its own, such as which specific stocks and bonds to buy, the fiduciary puts him or herself in direct competition with professional money managers and may be liable for the difference between the performance they generate and what a prudent expert may have generated.

2) Demonstrate that the prudent expert was selected by following a due-diligence process as described in Practices 3.4 and 4.4. This is very important. You must document *why* an expert was hired.

3) Give the prudent expert* discretion *over portfolio assets.

4) Have the prudent expert acknowledge its fiduciary status in writing. This is done by having the expert sign the investment policy statement (IPS), which must contain language that carefully spells out the expert's fiduciary duties. Mutual funds are governed by their respective prospectuses and are exempt from the need to sign the IPS.

5) Monitor the activities of the prudent expert to ensure that the expert is performing the agreed upon tasks. A prudent monitoring process is outlined in Practices 5.1 to 5.5.

The preceding five criteria established by the ERISA safe harbor rules that pertain to situations where investment decisions are made by an investment committee or investment adviser are relatively easy to implement.

The ERISA safe harbor rules that pertain to investment decisions made by participants in a retirement plan, however, are a tougher proposition. In the first place, these rules which are found in ERISA section 404(c) are simply *unknown* to many plan fiduciaries. Even when the sponsor of a 401(k) plan does know about them, many such sponsors are under the *mistaken impression* that if, for example, they provide plan participants with the ability to make their own investment decisions among at least three prudent and well-diversified investment options the sponsors are relieved of liability for any losses incurred by the plan participants. While these provisions are vitally important, they are only a few on a long list that must be implemented by an ERISA fiduciary in order to obtain section 404(c) relief from liability for the poor investment decisions made by plan participants.

The preamble to the ERISA 404(c) regulations explains the general requirements the sponsor of a qualified retirement plan must satisfy to merit 404(c) protection:

> In general, in order for a participant or beneficiary to exercise control over the assets in his account, the participant or beneficiary must have the opportunity, under the plan, to: (1) choose from a broad range of investment alternatives which consist of at least three diversified investment alternatives, each of which has materially different risk and return characteristics; (2) give investment instructions with a frequency which is appropriate in light of the market volatility of the investment alternatives, but not less frequently than once within any three-month period; (3) diversify investments within and among investment alternatives; and (4) obtain sufficient information to make informed investment decisions with respect to investment alternatives available under the plan.

However intricate the preceding four requirements may seem, securing 404(c) protection is actually even more complicated. The following is a list of additional requirements provided to me by Fred Reish, senior partner at the Los Angeles–based law firm of Reish Luftman Reicher & Cohen.

➢ Retirement plan participants must be notified in the "Summary Plan Document" that the plan intends to constitute a 404(c) plan.
➢ The participant must have an opportunity to obtain written confirmation of his instructions.
➢ The person to whom the instructions are given must be an identified plan fiduciary who is obligated to comply with the instructions.
➢ The participant must be provided with the following information *automatically* by an identified plan fiduciary:

1) An explanation that the plan is intended to be a 404(c) plan;

2) An explanation that the fiduciaries of the plan may be relieved of liability for losses;

3) A description of the investment alternatives available under the plan;

4) A general description of the investment objectives and risk and return characteristics of each designated alternative;

5) Identification of any designated investment managers;

6) An explanation about giving investment instructions;

7) A description of any transaction fees and expenses that affect the participant's account balance;

8) The name, address, and phone number of the plan fiduciary responsible for providing information;

9) Specified information regarding employer securities;

10) A copy of the most recent prospectus, either immediately before or after initial investment, provided to the plan for investment alternatives subject to the Securities Act of 1933; and

11) Any materials provided to the plan relating to the exercise of voting, tender or similar rights.

➢ The participant is able to obtain *upon request*:
  1) A description of the annual operating expenses of each designated investment alternative;
  2) Copies of any prospectuses, financial statements, and reports provided to the plan;
  3) A list of the assets comprising the portfolio of each designated investment alternative;
  4) Information concerning the value of shares or units in designated investment alternatives; and
  5) Information concerning the value of shares or units in designated investment alternatives held in the account of the participant.

➢ The Plan permits participants to give investment instructions with a frequency that is appropriate in light of market volatility.

➢ The core investment alternatives, constituting a broad range, permit instructions at least once within any three-month period.

Complying with Section 404(c) can seem like a monumental task to plan sponsors, to such an extent that some decide not to offer a retirement plan to their employees or consider terminating their existing plan because they fear liability. Moreover, many companies and organizations are understandably worried about unforeseen administrative burdens that could interfere with running their businesses, even though they may want to offer a quality retirement plan. Happily, that goal is more achievable than many plan sponsors think, once they understand what Section 404(c) does and does not require.

Understanding what is required is best accomplished by retaining an adviser knowledgeable in such matters. Many plan sponsors that wish to offer their employees a retirement plan turn to stockbrokers or insurance agents to help them set up a plan. These "service providers" no doubt are competent at providing such services. Those services, though, may come with some big risks that may not be known to a plan sponsor. That's why it is crucial for a sponsor to understand the real nature of its relationship with these service providers.

Any 401(k) plan must offer a menu of at least three investment options from which participants may select. The investment options offered by many stockbrokers and insurance agents in the plans they set up are supplied to them by firms such as mutual fund companies. A conflict of interest (or at the very least an appearance of one) is created when the firms offer to service providers a (often hefty) monetary incentive for using their particular investment options. The problem is that a plan sponsor can't ever really be sure whether the service provider is supplying quality investment options to the retirement plan or simply the investment options that give the provider the highest commission.

Plan sponsors should also be aware of the fact that stockbrokers and insurance agents are rarely designated as a "named" or "functional" fiduciary in retirement plan documents. A named or functional fiduciary becomes liable for certain aspects of the operation and administration of a retirement plan. Accepting legal status as a fiduciary responsible for certain functions, such as the selection and monitoring of investment options or Section 404(c) compliance, transfers some personal liability from the plan sponsor to the named or functional fiduciary. Many sponsors of retirement plans are misled into thinking that when a stockbroker or an insurance agent sets up a plan for them, the service provider becomes a fiduciary of the plan. That is almost never the case, though, with the result that no transfer of liability has occurred. That's why a plan sponsor should insist that any service provider claiming to be a fiduciary must clearly identify the specific functions they will perform and certify in writing, in accordance with ERISA law, that they will accept liability for that performed function.

One final note to all sponsors of retirement plans: the investment options offered in a retirement plan and the education provided by the plan sponsor must be geared toward the sophistication level of the plan's participants. You can provide very sophisticated investment options and advanced investment education to plan participants, but if they don't have the capacity to understand the information in order to make informed investment decisions, you may be breaching your fiduciary duties. I routinely counsel many participants after they have literally given up trying to make sense of the overwhelming amount of investment information that inundates them. In fact, very few participants in 401(k) plans have any understanding of concepts such as "standard deviation," "large cap," "small cap," "annual expense ratio," "turnover" or the "Sharpe ratio." Many participants do not even understand the basic differences between a stock and a bond. Your duty as a plan sponsor is not only to provide the information mandated by Section 404(c), but also to dispense it in such a way that plan participants can use it effectively. In short, keep it simple.

Practice 4.3: *Investment vehicles are appropriate for the portfolio size.*

Investors generally have three options when choosing investment vehicles. They can select specific stocks and bonds themselves. It is generally recommended that fiduciaries not do this, particularly those that are required to meet the ERISA prudent expert standard discussed in Practice 4.2.

The other two options include professionally managed mutual funds and separate accounts. The primary difference between the two is that mutual funds commingle the assets of many investors while separate accounts do not. There are no right and wrong answers for which investment vehicle to use. The Foundation for Fiduciary Studies suggests that mutual funds (including exchange-traded funds, or ETFs) be used for portfolios valued less than $1 million (it is difficult to achieve effective diversification with separate accounts for portfolios valued less than $1 million). The Foundation also recommends that a combination of mutual funds and separates accounts be used for portfolios valued between $1 million and $30 million, and separate accounts be used exclusively for portfolios valued at more than $30 million (separate accounts can be extremely cost efficient for portfolios at this asset level).

The Foundation provides some exceptions to the "over $30 million rule"; when a "passive" investment strategy is used and when the investor chooses to invest in stocks that have high trading costs such as emerging markets stocks, small company stocks, and micro stocks. If an investor wishes to follow a passive investment strategy, index funds or asset class funds are appropriate for any size portfolio. In fact, there are billion dollar–plus institutional portfolios that are invested primarily in passively managed mutual funds.

The following list, provided courtesy of the Foundation for Fiduciary Studies, outlines the benefits of mutual funds and separate accounts:

Benefits of mutual funds:

1) Greater liquidity, ease in entering and exiting
2) Requires smaller dollar amounts to open accounts
3) Ease in putting cash to work while money is in transition
4) Greater degree of diversification
5) Ease in meeting asset allocation and rebalancing guidelines
6) Ease in due diligence with databases

7) Information is required to be audited
8) Ease in implementing international portfolios
9) Greater cash flows may meet disbursement requirements
10) Fees may be netted from distributions, reducing taxable income

Benefits of separate accounts:
1) Can be funded with securities-in-kind, assets with low or preferred tax basis
2) Eliminates phantom tax consequences associated with funds
3) Permits for year-end tax harvesting
4) Easier to ascertain which securities are in the portfolio
5) Ease in reducing total fees as account size grows
6) Brokerage can be directed for soft dollar or commission recapture programs
7) Manager can be given specific securities guidelines, SRI
8) Management fees may be deductible

Fiduciaries need to be aware of and understand the difference between managed accounts and separate accounts. A *managed account* (a sort of separate account promoted by Wall Street brokerage firms) is known as a *wrap program.* This entails "wrapping" all the services provided by the firm into one fee, which includes the asset management fee, trading costs, performance reporting, and a fee for the broker/consultant. Brokerage firms pitch wrap programs to investors with as little as $25,000 to invest by promising them that they will have access to institutional money managers that ordinarily have multimillion-dollar investment minimums.

Investors should understand clearly the potential differences between how accounts are managed at the institutional level and at the wrap program level. For example, it is worthwhile to compare the difference in performance at the institutional level and the wrap program level to see if it is significant; often it is. It also should be determined whether the people managing at the institutional level are the same people managing at the wrap program level. In addition, the overall investment management process should be analyzed at both levels.

An effective way to analyze a wrap program when considering it for inclusion in a portfolio is to require that the brokerage firm provide performance data for existing wrap clients. In your analysis, be careful not to make decisions based on the composite reports provided by the brokerage firm or the money manager. If the broker/consultant pleads confidentiality, simply ask her to omit all client information from the performance reports. Be sure to get at least three years of actual client performance data.

The primary benefit of separate accounts is the ability to better customize a portfolio. Separate accounts enable investors to carry out very specific investment objectives. For example, excluding certain types of investments for an investor who wishes to implement a socially responsible investment strategy is best achieved through a separate account. An investor that has a low basis stock in its portfolio and wants to unwind (i.e., sell) it slowly can hire a sophisticated separate account manager to help do it in a tax-efficient manner. If an investor is holding a stock that comprises a large percentage of the total value of his portfolio and he wants to sell it (for estate, tax or other reasons), a separate account manager can be instructed to avoid adding any additional shares of that particular stock to the portfolio; this cannot be achieved through a mutual fund. Dealing with restricted stock positions also can be managed more effectively through a separate account.

In sum, separate accounts are appropriate for very large accounts and for investors wishing to carry out very specific investment objectives. Low-cost no-load mutual funds (including ETFs) are appropriate for investors with small, as well as large, portfolios who wish to implement passive investment strategies. As always, though, the unique facts and circumstances of each investor will help determine the proper investment vehicle to use.

Practice 4.4: *A due-diligence process is followed in selecting service providers, including the custodian.*

Hiring and monitoring service providers is a fiduciary function. There are many types of service providers, including the following for retirement plans: an auditor (for plans with 100 or more employees), trustee, custodian, record keeper, third-party administrator, investment managers (Practice 3.4 outlines an excellent selection and monitoring process for investment managers), and the adviser/consultant. Private trusts do not need as many service providers as retirement plans, but for any service provider that is hired, the need for a defined selection and monitoring process still applies. When considering many different providers, it is important for the fiduciary to supply all prospective providers with an identical request that outlines the type of account that is seeking service and what services are needed. The following are twelve excellent tips for selecting and monitoring service providers that was provided by the Employee Benefits Security Administration:

1) Consider what services you need for your plan; legal, accounting, trustee/custodial, record-keeping, investment management, investment education, or advice.

2) Ask Service providers about their services, experience with employee benefit plans, fees and expenses, customer references, or other information relating to the quality of their services and customer satisfaction with such services.

3) Present each prospective service provider identical and complete information regarding the needs of your plan. You may want to get formal bids from those providers that seem best suited to your needs.

4) You may also wish to consider service providers or alliances of providers who provide multiple services (e.g., custodial trustee, investment management, education, or advice, and record keeping) for a single fee. These arrangements are often called "bundled services."

5) Ask each prospective provider to be specific about which services are covered for the estimated fees and which are not. Compare the information you receive, including fees and expenses to be charged by the various providers for similar services. Note that plan fiduciaries are not always required to pick the least costly provider. Cost is only one factor to be considered in selecting a service provider. (Although it is short on its discussion regarding revenue sharing agreements, an excellent fee disclosure worksheet can be found on the DOL website at www.dol.gov/ebsa/pdf/401kfefm.pdf.)

6) If the service provider will handle plan assets, check to make sure that the provider has a fidelity bond (a type of insurance that protects the plan against loss resulting from fraudulent or dishonest acts).

7) If a service provider must be licensed (attorneys, accountants, investment managers, or advisers), check with state or federal licensing authorities to confirm the provider has an up-to-date license and whether there are any complaints against the provider.

8) Make sure you understand the terms of any agreements or contracts you sign with service providers and the fees and expenses associated with the contracts. In particular, understand what obligations both you and the service provider have under the agreement and whether the fees and expenses to be charged to you and plan participants are reasonable in light of the services to be provided.

9) Prepare a written record of the process you followed in reviewing potential service providers and the reasons for your selection of a particular provider. This record may be helpful in answering any future questions that may arise concerning your selection.

10) Receive a commitment from your service provider to regularly provide you with information regarding the services it provides.
11) Periodically review the performance of your service providers to ensure that they are proving the services in a manner and at a cost consistent with the agreements.
12) Review plan participant comments or any complaints about the services and periodically ask whether there have been any changes in the information you received from the service provider prior to hiring (e.g., does the provider continue to maintain any required state or federal licenses?).

Regarding records for retirement plan sponsors that are maintained by a third party. Do not assume you own the records; make sure in your contract with them it clearly states you as the plan sponsor "own" the records. Unfortunately, many plan sponsors have discovered that they did not own the records when they decided to terminate a particular service provider, which can make the transition to a new service provider very difficult. This is an important question that should be addressed in any selection process.

Step Five

Monitor and Supervise

Practices 5.1–5.5

Step Five is the most labor-intensive step of the five-step investment management process. Unlike Steps One through Four, which are reviewed primarily on an annual basis, Step Five requires quarterly work. Performance monitoring is complex and is where most of the problems within the investment management process occur. Step Five is where the "rubber meets the road" because it is at this point in the investment-management process wherein the conduct of all the parties involved is examined to see if it collectively measures up.

Practice 5.1: *Periodic reports compare investment performance against an appropriate index, peer group, and IPS objectives.*

While the term "periodic" is not defined, most experts agree that reports monitoring the progress of an investment program should be prepared at least quarterly. The primary report is the performance report. The primary report as well as other reports should provide an investor with the following minimum amount of information while at the same time ensuring proper monitoring:

➢ The returns of the major asset classes for the past quarter; year-to-date; and one-, three-, and five-year periods;
➢ The performance of the account at the portfolio level for the periods of quarter to date, year to date, and inception to date;
➢ A comparison of the account performance to an appropriate benchmark portfolio;
➢ A comparison of the current asset allocation versus the target allocation outlined in the IPS; and
➢ A comparison of the individual funds or managers to an appropriate benchmark.

The preceding information can be used to answer the following questions:

➢ Is the overall portfolio performance satisfactory based on the target allocation?
➢ Is rebalancing needed?
➢ Should any investment options be replaced?
➢ Are the objectives outlined in the IPS being met?
➢ Is there a need for a change in the target allocation? This would happen only if there was a change in the investor's risk tolerance. It is important to understand that significant events occurring in financial markets should not dictate changes in an investor's portfolio asset allocation. Only events in an investor's personal life, such as radical changes in need for income or other such circumstances, should cause changes in the investor's asset allocation.

I provide my clients with the preceding information every quarter to ensure that each question has been asked and answered. In addition, I provide the latest quarterly performances of the major market indexes as shown in the table on pages 154–155, "Quarterly Market Review."

This information gives an investor a good overall perspective on how the financial markets have performed. I then compare such data to what the investor actually experienced.

I review each investor's performance report before it is sent. Because the investment industry makes things more complicated than they need to be, I try to make this exercise as simple as possible. Investors are interested in the bottom line and whether or not they need to make any adjustments to the portfolio. They do not want complicated risk/return scatter grams and the like. The figure on page 156, "Performance Analysis," shows an investor's portfolio performance for the following periods: latest quarter (third quarter 2004), year to date, previous two calendar years and inception to date; this shows the bottom line. (This is an actual client account of Hatton Consulting, Inc., with an inception date of May 18, 2000.) The figure "Determining Need for Rebalancing," on page 157, compares the actual allocation (current market values) to the target allocation (allocation agreed upon and written in IPS); this helps to determine whether adjustments to the portfolio are needed.

On the Performance Analysis you can see the stamp I use to communicate with the client. This lets them know I have reviewed the account and, in this case, have determined no adjustments are needed. I came to this conclusion by first reviewing the account by comparing its performance to the 60/40 benchmark portfolio (default portfolio), which has been imported into the report. The client portfolio returned 0.51% for the quarter and 4.81% year to date compared to 0.17% and 3.32% respectively for the benchmark portfolio. For the calendar years of 2003 and 2002, the client portfolio returned 25.85% and –6.60%, respectively, versus 24.04% and –7.05% for the benchmark portfolio. Finally, and in my opinion most importantly because it is the longest measurement period, the inception-to-date performance is compared. You can see the client portfolio has an annualized

Quarterly Market Review

ASSET CLASS	SHORT-TERM BONDS	INTERMEDIATE BONDS	LARGE-CAP STOCKS
Index	Leh Bros 1–3 Yr	Leh Bros Inter	S&P 500
QTD	1.0	2.8	1.6
YTD	1.0	2.8	1.6
One Year	2.4	7.4	35.1
Three-Year Annualized	4.9	8.5	0.6
Five-Year Annualized	5.6	7.8	−1.2
2003	2.0	6.8	28.6
2002	6.0	10.1	−22.0
2001	8.5	9.7	−11.8
2000	8.1	9.4	−9.1
1999	2.9	0.1	21.0

Note: Data for the period ending March 31, 2004.

Source: Morningstar Principia and Fiduciary Analytics

return of 6.22% since May 18, 2000, versus 4.29% for the benchmark portfolio.

A word of caution: It is inadequate to compare actual non-risk-adjusted performance to benchmarks to determine whether a portfolio is performing satisfactorily based only on this comparison. There are circumstances that should not alarm investors if their portfolio performance is lagging a benchmark portfolio. For instance, the duration of a client bond portfolio may be either longer or shorter than a benchmark portfolio; if this is the case, the performance will differ. This comparison is only one piece in the performance evaluation pie. Other factors need to be addressed, such as the appropriateness of the benchmark, portfolio volatility, and the time period being measured. Quarterly performance needs to be monitored, but much

INTERNATIONAL STOCKS	SMALL-CAP STOCKS	REAL ESTATE INVESTMENT TRUSTS	INFLATION
MSCI EAFE ND	Russell 2000	Wilshire REIT	CPI
4.3	6.0	12.0	1.0
4.3	6.0	12.0	1.0
57.5	63.5	50.6	1.0
3.4	10.8	21.4	1.8
0.5	9.6	18.7	2.4
38.5	47.2	36.0	1.8
−15.9	−20.4	3.6	2.3
−21.4	2.4	12.3	1.5
−14.1	−3.0	31.0	3.3
26.9	21.2	−2.5	2.6

longer time periods need to be studied before final conclusions are drawn because, especially in the short run, any well-constructed portfolio may experience periods of underperformance relative to benchmarks.

The figure on page 157, "Determining Need for Rebalancing," shows the actual versus target allocation. The "percent variance" column indicates all asset classes are within the stated trading range (which is stated in the IPS to be 25% from the target in either direction). Investors want to know that their investments are being monitored. This report is clear evidence that quarterly monitoring is taking place and makes it easier for the client to understand why changes to the portfolio may be made. For instance, this particular investor has a target allocation of 15% for short-term high-quality fixed income.

Performance Analysis

05/31/2000–09/30/2004	
Beginning Value	1,034,591.57
Contributions	674.57
Withdrawals	0
Capital Appreciation	155,309.18
Income/Expenses	155,399.72
Ending Value	1,345,975.06
Investment Gain	310,708.92

TOTAL PORTFOLIO	3RD QUARTER	YTD	2003	2002	INCEPTION
Time Weighted (net)	0.51	4.81	25.85	−6.60	6.22
60/40	0.34	3.32	24.04	−7.05	4.29
Difference	0.17	1.49	1.81	0.45	1.93

Returns for periods exceeding 12 months are annualized.
All returns net of fees.

Reviewed By: T. H.
Required Action This Quarter:
- ☐ Rebalance
- ☐ Investment Option Replacement
- ☐ Asset Allocation Adjustment
- ☒ None
- ☐ Other

A 25% deviation above or below the target sets a trading range of approximately 11.25% to 18.75% (plus or minus 3.75% from the target of 15%). The client understands, because of the detailed discussion we have had about the rebalancing process, I may suggest a sell if the allocation to short-term high-quality fixed income has risen to 18.75%, or I may suggest a buy if the allocation has fallen to 11.25%; the current allocation is 11.9%,

Determining Need for Rebalancing

Asset allocation as of 09/30/2004

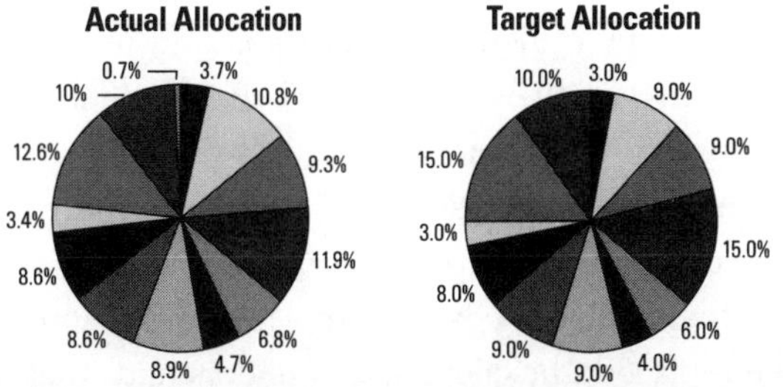

DESCRIPTION	WEIGHT	CURRENT VALUE	TARGET PERCENT	TARGET VALUE	DOLLAR VARIANCE	PERCENT VARIANCE
Cash & Equivalent	0.7%	9,694.92	0.0	0.00	−9,694.92	−0.7
High-Yield Fixed Income	10.0%	134,303.20	10.0	134,597.51	294.31	0.0
Intermediate-Term High-Quality F	12.6%	169,860.88	15.0	201,896.26	32,035.38	2.4
Large Blend Emerging Int'l	3.4%	46,153.71	3.0	40,379.25	−5,774.46	−0.4
Large Blend International	8.6%	115,572.75	8.0	107,678.00	−7,894.75	−0.6
Large-Cap Blend	8.6%	115,181.51	9.0	121,137.76	5,956.25	0.4
Large-Cap Value	8.9%	119,529.32	9.0	121,137.76	1,608.44	0.1
Large Value International	4.7%	62,994.21	4.0	53,839.00	−9,155.21	−0.7
Real Estate	6.8%	92,090.24	6.0	80,758.50	−11,331.74	−0.8
Short-Term High-Quality Fixed In	11.9%	160,182.85	15.0	201,896.26	41,713.41	3.1
Small-Cap Blend	9.3%	125,343.15	9.0	121,137.76	−4,205.39	−0.3
Small-Cap Value	10.8%	145,808.10	9.0	121,137.76	−24,670.34	−1.8
Small Value International	3.7%	49,260.22	3.0	40,379.25	−8,880.97	−0.7
	100.0%	1,345,975.06	100.0	1,345,975.06		

Source: Hatton Consulting, Inc.

which remains within the hold range. This is a disciplined process of buying low and selling high.

Determining whether an investment option needs to be replaced is done by utilizing the selection and monitoring process outlined in Practices 3.4 and 3.5. If a fund has been on "watch" status and it becomes time to sell the fund, I will check the "investment option replacement" box. Like the rebalancing process, the client is aware of the termination process *before* the time comes that a fund needs to be replaced. Therefore, if a fund needs to be replaced, the client clearly understands that the decision was made within the framework of a predetermined objective process and, as a result, does not question the action.

Finally, an objective outlined in this client's IPS was for the investor's portfolio is to perform 3 percent over inflation. The reports I have provided the client indicate this objective has been met. Determining whether an objective has been met must also be done within an appropriate time horizon. At a minimum, a full market cycle, three to five years, should be allowed to elapse before determining whether the objective has been realized.

Practice 5.2: *Periodic reviews are made of qualitative and/or organizational changes of investment decision makers.*

I have already defined quantitative criteria for evaluating money managers through the due-diligence process. However, the analysis also should include qualitative measures. The following are seven recommended qualitative criteria to include in the analysis:

- ➢ Staff turnover
- ➢ Organizational structure
- ➢ Investment philosophy

- Level of service provided, including the quality of responses to requests for information
- Quality of reports
- Investment process
- Legal, SEC, or regulatory proceedings or actions

There are a number of quality money management firms both at the mutual fund level and at the separate account level. One firm that has extremely low staff turnover is the American Funds Group. The portfolio managers at this family of mutual funds average twenty-three years of investment experience, twenty of which are with the American Funds Group. During the investment mania of the late 1990s, it was estimated that the average *age* of a portfolio manager was twenty-nine! Experience and low staff turnover are excellent qualitative measures to review.

The organizational structure of a money manager is also very important to understand. In the case of a mutual fund, for example, is the fund owned by public shareholders, privately owned, or owned by the fund's shareholders? To my knowledge, the Vanguard Group is the only fund group where the shareholders of the funds actually own the funds. Vanguard provides the investment management and services to fund shareholders on an "at-cost" basis. This is the primary reason why Vanguard is able to manage its mutual funds at such low costs. In my opinion, there is no question that the interests of fund shareholders come first at Vanguard.

Another recommended qualitative criterion to include in the analysis of a money management firm is the investment philosophy of the firm. Does the firm believe in an active or passive money management philosophy or provide both? Is the firm a value or growth manager? Does it favor large company or small company stocks? If the firm invests in international stocks, does it use currency hedging? Is a commitment to low fees a priority? It is very important to understand a firm's commitment to its stated investment philosophy. Studying the firm's past performance in different market cycles will shed light on that commitment. For example, the performance of small company value managers was virtually zero in the late 1990s. Many firms "cheated" as a result by purchasing more growth-oriented stocks, which ultimately hurt their performances. More important, though, such cheating signaled a weakness in the firms' commitment to their investment philosophy.

What is the level and types of services the firm provides and how does it respond to requests for information? Is it a small boutique firm specializing in small company stocks or a large mutual fund complex offering a multitude of services such as online trading, retirement plan services, high-net-worth services, financial planning, cash management, and the like? What is the firm's experience in each of the areas it offers services? Does the firm respond in a timely manner to any requests for information? Has there been a change in the firm's response time and attitude? Is there online access to information? One of the most important things I look for at any firm I work with is a specific contact person that I can get to know. I do not (and likely neither does anyone else) want to deal with an automated voice response system! I find it to be an excellent indication of a firm's commitment to high-level service if it is willing to spend what it takes to provide truly personal contact.

Does the investment firm provide timely and quality reports? I want quickly to be able to get (among other information) performance, tax, dividend, cost, and other data. You should be able to access this information online.

Is the firm's investment process transparent? Does it keep its investment process a secret or does it bring it to light and openly educate? My experience in the investment advisory profession has been that the more education the better the investment experience. Dimensional Fund Advisors, the Vanguard Group, the American Funds Group, and separate account managers such as Brandes Partners and Parametric, demonstrate an ongoing commitment to education that benefits all parties involved. Quality education can be delivered through a number of means, including conferences, newsletters, online information, and printed research reports.

The mutual fund scandals uncovered in 2003 and 2004 dealt a real blow to investor confidence. Fiduciaries should obviously take into consideration all legal and regulatory proceedings against investment firms in their decision-making process. I believe it is important to try and ascertain *who* within an accused firm is responsible or even involved. Was the behavior an isolated incident involving one or a few employees or was it a high-level, systematic problem? As previously noted, Putnam Funds was one firm implicated in these scandals and it was reported the problems were not isolated but part of the corporate culture. How did the firm respond to the allegations? Was the response swift and complete or delayed in some way? Were there any changes at the firm as a result of the allegations, such as levying a sales charge on international funds for redemptions made within a short time horizon in an effort to combat late trading? Edward D. Jones & Co. was accused of receiving an estimated $100 million a year from Putnam (and more from other mutual fund families) in exchange for unduly favoring Putnam funds at the expense of non-Putnam funds. That is, Putnam and Edward D. Jones & Co. engaged in a "pay to play" scheme in which Putnam paid Jones to push its funds, and Jones responded by selling those funds to the exclusion of others that may have been more appropriate investments for Jones' customers. In fact, it is illegal for brokerage firms to receive payments from mutual fund companies in exchange for including the companies' funds in the brokers' arsenal of investment products *unless the receipt of such payments is fully disclosed to investors and the funds merit inclusion on the basis of an objective due-diligence process.*

As a response to the scandals in the mutual fund industry, Fiduciary Analytics has developed the Mutual Fund Family Fiduciary Rankings™. Mutual fund families are ranked according to the percentage of individual funds, with a time since inception date greater than three years, that pass the due-diligence process that I outlined in Practice 3.4. For example, for the period ending March 31, 2004, the Vanguard Group (85 percent of funds passed), the American Funds Group (59.6 percent of funds passed), and Dimensional Fund Advisors (52.5 percent of funds passed) all landed in the top ranking quartile. Putnam (23 percent of funds passed) landed in the third quartile. These rankings revealed that an overwhelming majority of fund families implicated in the fund scandals did not rank in the top ranking quartile. This system is not a panacea, but it is a good tool to help a fiduciary identify potential problems at a particular mutual fund family.

Practice 5.3: *Control procedures are in place to periodically review policies for best execution, soft dollars, and proxy voting.*

In the investment industry, the term "best execution" refers to the process of obtaining the best trading price for a given security that's available in any market trading the security. After a review of the rules of the Securities and Exchange Commission, Department of Labor regulations, as well as a number of other sources of information, I have found that there is no uniform and clear definition of best execution.

Best execution does not simply mean that an investor receives the highest price possible when selling or that it pays the lowest price possible when buying. Other factors, such as the speed of execution and the role of market impact costs, are also involved.

The process of best execution is full of potential conflicts of interest. Stockbrokers can route trades for execution to an exchange, a market maker, or an electronic communications network (ECNs), or they can even internalize trades (fill orders from their own inventory to possibly make additional money on the "spread"). A conflict of interest can arise, for example, when a stockbroker receives "payment for order flow" and then directs trades to specific exchanges, market makers, or ECNs. This practice is not illegal as long as the quality of execution is not sacrificed. The problem, though, is that it is virtually impossible to determine whether or not best execution on a particular trade has actually occurred.

Managers of separate accounts and mutual funds must direct their trades to brokers for execution. Fiduciaries need to monitor how these managers direct trades. One way to do this is to obtain the written procedures for best execution policies from managers of separate accounts and mutual funds. These procedures should show how the managers determine what brokers they will use to make trades. The problem, though, again is that it is nearly impossible to determine whether the managers of mutual funds and separate accounts are, in fact, getting best execution.

For mutual funds, a better way of determining whether best execution has occurred may come from studying the performance of a mutual fund relative to its peer group and benchmark. Executing trades is a cost to a mutual fund and, generally speaking, funds with low overall costs tend to be among the best performers. Mutual funds with lower overall costs, then, are more likely to experience best execution. For separate accounts, there is more transparency in determining best execution because the custodial statements will show which brokers were used and the execution price of each trade.

Soft dollars can be defined as services of value provided to the order giver (management firm), by the order taker (wire house) in exchange for the order. These services are provided out of the "excess profit" earned on the trade by the order taker (the difference between what a stockbrokerage firm charges a customer for trading a stock and the actual cost to the firm of making the trade). There is nothing illegal about "overpaying" for the trade, as long as the customer whose account is affected benefits, directly or indirectly, from the soft dollar benefits provided to the order giver. In essence, the customer is overcharged on the trade (relative to cheaper available alternatives) in exchange for services provided to the customer or the customer's manager or fund. These services can include research, technology, or other assistance. I do not believe this practice will be allowed to continue in its present form for much longer in the current regulatory environment. This may, however, be just wishful thinking.

As mentioned, one service that is often purchased with soft dollars is investment research. Abuses can occur when an adviser/consultant is improperly induced to direct business to brokerages firms or fund companies in order to purchase investment research. In return for that business, the brokerages or fund companies provide gifts, lavish trips, computers, or other incentives to the adviser/consultant all under the guise that these gifts somehow benefit the customer. All managers of separate accounts and mutual funds should have written guidelines in place for soft dollars. If soft dollars are used, a written agreement detailing the amount and use of should be maintained. Some money managers make it a business practice not to engage in the use of soft dollars; this should be encouraged by the fiduciary advisers.

With respect to proxy voting, proxies should be voted in a way that best enhances the stock's value for the shareholder (i.e., customer). Money managers must take this responsibility seriously. They should outline their policies in regard to when and why they may vote for or against management and shareholder initiatives. A proxy log must be kept in order to detail how the money manager voted in all cases and it must be made available to all clients upon request.

For mutual funds, information on best execution, soft dollar, and proxy voting policies may be found in the prospectus or Statement of Additional Information (SAI). If this information cannot be found in these documents, contact the mutual fund company and ask how to obtain it. Separate account managers should provide such information upon request. I would avoid doing business with any mutual fund or separate account that has inadequate written policies and procedures covering these three issues.

Practice 5.4: *Fees for investment management are consistent with agreements and the law.*

An adviser should help a fiduciary ensure that:

- Fees can be paid from portfolio assets (i.e., ERISA accounts);
- Fees are appropriate and reasonable for the services being provided; and
- Fees actually charged to clients are in accordance with the formulas in written agreements that are used to calculate those fees.

Any fee that is imposed on the assets of an ERISA plan must result in a direct benefit to the plan beneficiaries. Such fees would include those incurred for selection and monitoring of investment options and investment management fees. There are some gray areas, however. For example, the Department of Labor (DOL) has classified certain activities as "settlor" functions. One settlor function identified by the DOL involves the fees spent on plan design studies. Because these fees are incurred during the "formation" of a retirement plan before its adoption, the DOL has taken the position that such fees may not be passed on to the plan in the future. Given the highly technical nature of this area, I recommend that you consult with an experienced ERISA attorney if there are any doubts whether or not a specific service directly benefits plan participants and thus can be charged to them.

Fiduciaries must also determine if fees charged are appropriate and reasonable. There are no clear-cut guidelines, as noted, for determining what is "appropriate" or "reasonable." For non-ERISA accounts, I suggest making a comparison between the cost of the services for which the client is actually being charged and the average cost of those services charged by other similar investment managers. The actual cost charged the investor should bear close scrutiny if he is being charged significantly in excess of the average cost. In Practice 3.6, I estimated that reasonable costs for the entire investment management process should not exceed 1.7 percent of assets under management. I recommend that the four primary components of fees—money management, trading, custody, and adviser/consulting—should be broken down and analyzed thoroughly. This is essential because it is difficult to see how an adviser can help a fiduciary determine whether or not fees charged are appropriate and reasonable if the adviser cannot understand who is being paid for what and in what amount. The analysis is helpful in exposing possible excess charges.

The Employee Benefits Security Administration (EBSA, which is part of the DOL) has published a useful report entitled *Study of 401(k) Plan Fees and Expenses.*[5] You can access it online at http://www.dol.gov/ebsa. The study is an excellent resource for fiduciaries of ERISA retirement plans and I highly recommend it. It provides an overview of fees and trends within the retirement plan market and should be a big help to fiduciaries in determining the reasonableness of fees. However, it does not identify sub-T.A. (sub-transfer agent) fees or break out 12b-1 fees; it is crucial that these fees be identified.

Checks and balances must be put into place to ensure that the fees actually charged to clients are in accordance with the formulas in written agreements that are used to calculate those fees. To reiterate, I recommend that the four primary components of fees—money management, trading, custodial, and adviser/consulting—should be broken down. Investors should identify these four components and record in one place who is providing each of the services and the amount of the agreed upon fees. Most fees for money management accounts are deducted on a quarterly basis in the month following the end of a quarter and are found in the custodial statement. Fees for the broker/consultant, custodian, and separate account manager are usually identified on the custodial statement. Trading fees are identified on the trading slip confirmations. Mutual fund fees appear in annual reports, which should be read in conjunction with the prospectus. I also recommend that the Statement of Additional Information be reviewed periodically since it outlines all aspects of the management of a mutual fund. Nothing, though, can really substitute for sitting down and manually checking each fee charged to ensure that it is in accord with the formulas described in written agreements. After all, mistakes do occur, and the quicker they are identified the quicker they can be rectified.

Practice 5.5: *"Finders fees," 12b-1 fees, or other forms of compensation that have been paid for asset placement are appropriately applied, utilized, and documented.*

There are few things more convoluted than the compensation structures in the financial industry. A lack of transparency and secrecy is the norm. When you know what to look for, however, it is relatively easy to determine who is being paid for what. For example, one form of a commission is a finder's fee. The most common finder's fee is when an adviser/broker receives a commission for placing assets, usually $1 million or more, with a particular mutual fund company. Once the $1 million minimum is met, the investor is able to buy fund shares at the net asset value (NAV); this makes it seem that the investor can invest without paying a commission. However, the mutual fund company actually pays the adviser/broker $10,000 (a 1 percent commission on the $1 million investment), yet there is no direct disclosure to the investor. If the investor wishes to sell the assets within twelve months, he is then saddled with a 1 percent deferred commission charge. While there is nothing wrong with this arrangement, it must be disclosed to the investor.

A particular source of confusion regarding compensation in the financial industry is the utilization of multiple mutual fund share classes, particularly Class B shares. This class of shares does not impose an up-front sales charge, even though the adviser/broker does receive an up-front commission. The investor should be told the specific reasons why the adviser/broker is choosing Class B shares and that there may be a charge when selling them. In addition, in the numerous retirement plan proposals I have reviewed, invariably I find the plan sponsor is given an "average fund expense ratio" that represents their disclosure of fund fees and then find when it is time for specific recommendations that B, C, and R shares are utilized (these share classes generally have the highest expense ratios). This practice can significantly understate the true cost to a retirement plan.

The area where the lack of transparency in the financial industry's compensation structure is greatest is in employee retirement plans. Sponsors of retirement plans are often told that many services they receive from plan providers are free. That assertion is demonstrably untrue. In one way or another, every provider of services to a retirement plan is being paid. Sub-T.A. fees, a form of revenue-sharing, are paid when a mutual fund company kicks back a portion of its management fees to pay for record-keeping or other services. Sub-T.A. fees are often misrepresented or not disclosed. Because they are used to offset administration and record-keeping fees, many plan sponsors are led to believe they are receiving these services at very little or no cost to the plan. Again, there is nothing wrong with this practice if the fees are fully disclosed. If you are a plan sponsor, always ask for all revenue-sharing arrangements in writing. If you are told there are none, get that fact in writing as well.

There are also forms of indirect revenue sharing. An example of this is an adviser/broker that receives trips, conferences, dinners, or other forms of indirect compensation by steering plan assets to certain mutual fund companies or separate account managers. Another example of indirect revenue sharing can be found when a parent company owns both a pension consulting firm and a mutual fund company. Economic benefit occurs when the pension consulting firm recommends to a plan sponsor investment in the funds of the mutual fund company owned by the same parent company; that recommendation is obviously a potential conflict of interest. Fiduciaries also need to be aware of all fees associated with the management of portfolio assets, including 12b-1 fees. The best way to achieve this, in my opinion, is to hire an independent, qualified outside consultant that is experienced in uncovering and describing all fees, both disclosed and undisclosed. It is important to understand that such consultants should be paid only by a plan sponsor.

I have paid a lot of attention to fees and disclosures in the preceding Practices. I would now like to cover 12b-1 fees, which are a hotly contested and controversial issue. Lori Walsh, a staff economist with the SEC, is the author of an article titled "The Cost and Benefits to Fund Shareholders of 12b-1 Plans: An Examination of Fund Flows, Expenses and Returns." Walsh observes: "Rule

12b-1, promulgated pursuant to the Investment Company Act of 1940, allows mutual fund advisers to make payments from fund assets for the costs of marketing and distribution of fund shares under the auspices of 12b-1 plans. The original justification for the plans, as put forth by the mutual fund industry in the 1970s, was that such fees help attract new shareholders into funds through advertising and by providing incentives for brokers to market the fund. Arguably, asset growth from any means benefits shareholders through economies of scale in management expenses and lower flow volatility, which decreases liquidity costs for the fund. If, through 12b-1 plans, funds are able to increase the rate at which their assets grow, then shareholders may be able to attain these cost reductions sooner than by investing in a fund with no 12b-1 plan. However, the costs must decrease sufficiently to cover the cost of the plan, and the benefits of the cost reductions must be passed onto shareholders, or shareholders will not be better off."

Walsh concludes: "If 12b-1 plans constitute a net benefit to investors, the amount of the annual fee should be recovered through higher net returns. Higher net returns could derive from either lower expense ratios due to economies of scale or higher gross returns due to the enhanced capacity of funds to either invest in assets with higher yields or reduce transactions costs. *Overall, the results are inconsistent with this hypothesis. 12b-1 plans do seem to be successful in growing fund assets, but with no apparent benefits accruing to the shareholders of the fund* [emphasis added]. Although it is hypothetically possible for most types of funds to generate sufficient scale economies to offset the 12b-1 fee, it is not an efficient use of shareholder assets. No shareholder will be better off investing in a small 12b-1 fund in hopes of helping the fund grow to attain these scale economies...Furthermore, these higher expenses do not translate into higher gross returns."

In my opinion, any fees in the investment management business that are not completely transparent should be avoided. Fiduciaries are required to know that 12b-1 fees exist and what services those fees are paying for. This is not to say, however, that there are not honest advisers who use funds with 12b-1 fees and fully disclose them and/or apply them appropriately. Nonetheless, far too many brokers/consultants do not disclose the fact they receive 12b-1 fees when in fact those fees could be used to offset other fees.

Another interesting case currently making its way through the federal courts involves a fund company that charges a 12b-1 fee to shareholders of funds that are closed to new shareholders. If the fund is closed to new investors, why should the fund collect a fee used to pay for expenses of acquiring new shareholders? The outcome of this case may have far-reaching implications as to the future appropriateness of 12b-1 fees.

This again brings us back to the need to break down fees so that an investor can clearly identify each fee charged and match it up to the service within the investment management process that is rendered for that fee. Only then can an adviser help the fiduciary determine if the fees being charged are appropriate and reasonable which, after all, is the ultimate goal in the analysis of fees. In the end, it is all about disclosure, disclosure, and more disclosure.

Conclusion

There are a number of benefits that result from implementing the foregoing twenty-seven Practices. Employing the Practices in a methodical way may help reduce liability by uncovering poor fiduciary practices that can lead to investor complaints. In the current environment of heightened legal scrutiny, utilizing a well-defined process is the wisest approach for fiduciaries to ensure that they are fulfilling their duties and responsibilities. The Practices also provide an excellent educational guideline that describes how the interests of all the parties involved in the investment and management of portfolio assets are aligned.

Long-term investment performance should also improve. This is accomplished by establishing procedures for diversifying the portfolio, selecting investment managers, terminating investment managers, monitoring performance, and accounting for investment fees and expenses. In addition, the Practices create an investment process standard. This standard, once adopted by the investment community, will be improved constantly by the collective efforts of those that most actively embrace it. As this process standard takes hold within the investment community, the investing public will come to realize how valuable it can be. Once investors understand that, they will seek out advisers that embrace this standard of care because they know it will result in the kind of advice that never compromises their interests.

Appendix I

Sample Investment Policy Statements

The following two investment policy statements are templates for an individual and a defined contribution plan; they were provided by the Center for Fiduciary Studies. To see these and other investment policy statement examples, visit their website at fi360.com.

INVESTMENT POLICY STATEMENT
High-Net-Worth Individual/Family Wealth (Client)
Approved on July 1, 2003

This investment policy statement should be reviewed and updated at least annually. Any change to this policy should be communicated in writing on a timely basis to all interested parties.

This Investment Policy Statement (IPS) has been prepared by Fiduciary Analytics. It is intended to serve as an example of the type of information that would be included in a comprehensive IPS. Clients are advised to have legal counsel review their IPS before it is approved.

EXECUTIVE SUMMARY

Type of Plan: Taxable, Individual
Current Assets: $650,000
Time Horizon: Greater than 5 years
Modeled Return: 7.28% (5.28% over the Consumer Price Index)
Modeled Loss: –9.39% (Probability level of 5%)
Asset Allocation:

	LOWER LIMIT	STRATEGIC ALLOCATION	UPPER LIMIT
Domestic Large-Cap Equity			
Blend	5%	10%	15%
Growth	5	10	15
Value	5	10	15
Mid-Cap Equity	5	10	15
Small-Cap Equity	5	10	15
International Equity	5	10	15
Intermediate-Term Fixed Income	30	35	40
Cash Equivalent	0	5	10

Evaluation Benchmarks:

Wealth Counseling Index™ (% Equity Exposure)*

	LCB	LCG	LCV	MCB	SCB	IE	IB	SB	MM
WCI (20)	5	5	5	0	0	5	40	30	10
WCI (40)	10	10	10	0	5	5	35	20	5
WCI (60)	10	10	10	10	10	10	35	0	5
WCI (80)	15	15	15	10	10	15	15	0	5

*The WCI™ series of indexes have several unique design features, two of which are:

1) They illustrate a series of prudently diversified portfolios; and
2) They illustrate the performance of a diversified portfolio, calculated using the performance of the median mutual fund manager for each peer group represented in the allocation.

PURPOSE

The purpose of this Investment Policy Statement (IPS) is to assist the Client and Investment Advisor (Advisor) in effectively supervising, monitoring and evaluating the investment of the Client's Portfolio (Portfolio). The Client's investment program is defined in the various sections of the IPS by:

1) Stating in a written document the Client's attitudes, expectations, objectives and guidelines for the investment of all assets.

2) Setting forth an investment structure for managing the Client's Portfolio. This structure includes various asset classes, investment management styles, asset allocation and acceptable ranges that, in total, are expected to produce an appropriate level of overall diversification and total investment return over the investment time horizon.

3) Encouraging effective communications between the Client and the Advisor.

4) Establishing formal criteria to select, monitor, evaluate and compare the performance of money managers on a regular basis.

5) Complying with all applicable fiduciary, prudence and due diligence requirements experienced investment professionals would utilize, and with all applicable laws, rules and regulations from various local, state, federal and international political entities that may impact the Client's assets.

BACKGROUND

This IPS has been prepared for John and Mary HNW Client (Client), a taxable entity. The assets covered by this IPS currently total approximately $650,000 in market value, but the Client's net worth is estimated to be

$1,225,000. Assets not covered by this IPS include:

1) Corporate sponsored defined contribution programs where both the husband and wife participate (combined, valued at $350,000); and

2) A vacation condo valued at $225,000.

Key Information

SSN: ______________________________

Investment Advisor: ______________________________

Additional key information, which is subject to change from time-to-time, is contained in Annex ___ (the appropriate annex).

STATEMENT OF OBJECTIVES

This IPS describes the prudent investment process the Advisor deems appropriate for the Client's situation. The Client desires to maximize returns within prudent levels of risk and to meet the following stated investment objectives:

Advisor lists investment objectives...

1) Retire with sufficient assets to support a lifestyle of __________.

2) Provide college tuition to grand children, etc.

Time Horizon

The investment guidelines are based upon an investment horizon of greater than five years; therefore interim fluctuations should be viewed with appropriate perspective. Short-term liquidity requirements are anticipated to be minimal.

Risk Tolerances

The Client recognizes and acknowledges some risk must be assumed in order to achieve long-term investment objectives, and there are uncertainties and complexities associated with contemporary investment markets.

In establishing the risk tolerances for this IPS, the Client's ability to withstand short and intermediate term variability was considered. The Client's prospects for the future, current financial condition, and several other factors suggest collectively some interim fluctuations in market value and rates of return may be tolerated in order to achieve the longer-term objectives.

Expected Return

In general, the Client would like the assets to earn at least a targeted return of 7.28%. It is understood an average return of 7.28% will require superior manager performance to: (1) retain principal value; and, (2) purchasing power. Furthermore, the objective is to earn a long-term rate of return at least 5.28% greater than the rate of inflation as measured by the Consumer Price Index (CPI).

Asset Class Preferences

The Client understands long-term investment performance, in large part, is primarily a function of asset class mix. The Client has reviewed the long-term performance characteristics of the broad asset classes, focusing on balancing the risks and rewards.

History shows while interest-generating investments, such as bond portfolios, have the advantage of relative stability of principal value, they provide little opportunity for real long-term capital growth due to their susceptibility to inflation. On the other hand, equity investments, such as common stocks, clearly have a significantly higher expected return but have the disadvantage of much greater year-by-year variability of return. From an investment decision-making point of view, this year-by-year variability may be worth accepting, provided the time horizon for the equity portion of the portfolio is sufficiently long (five years or greater).

The performance expectations (both risk and return) of each asset class are contained in Annex A. The following eight asset classes were selected and ranked in ascending order of "risk" (least to most): Money Market (MM), Intermediate Bond (IB), Large Cap Value (LCV), Large Cap Blend (LCB), Large Cap Growth (LCG), Mid Cap Blend (MCB), Small Cap Blend (SCB), International Equity (IE).

The Client has considered the following asset classes for inclusion in the asset mix, but has decided to exclude these asset classes at the present time: Global Fixed Income, Real Estate.

Rebalancing of Strategic Allocation

The percentage allocation to each asset class may vary as much as plus or minus 5% depending upon market conditions. When necessary and/or available, cash inflows/outflows will be deployed in a manner consistent with the strategic asset allocation of the Portfolio. If there are no cash flows, the allocation of the Portfolio will be reviewed quarterly.

If the Advisor judges cash flows to be insufficient to bring the Portfolio within the strategic allocation ranges, the Client shall decide whether to effect transactions to bring the strategic allocation within the threshold ranges (Strategic Allocation).

DUTIES AND RESPONSIBILITIES

Investment Advisor

The Client has retained an objective, third-party Advisor to assist the Client in managing the investments. The Advisor will be responsible for guiding the Client through a disciplined and rigorous investment process. As a fiduciary to the Client, the primary responsibilities of the Advisor are:

1) Prepare and maintain this investment policy statement.

2) Provide sufficient asset classes with different and distinct risk/return profiles so the Client can prudently diversify the Portfolio.

3) Prudently select investment options.

4) Control and account for all investment expenses.

5) Monitor and supervise all service vendors and investment options.

6) Avoid prohibited transactions and conflicts of interest.

Investment Managers

As distinguished from the Advisor, who is responsible for *managing* the investment process, investment managers are responsible for *making* investment decisions (security selection and price decisions). The specific duties and responsibilities of each investment manager are:

1) Manage the assets under their supervision in accordance with the guidelines and objectives outlined in their respective Service Agreements, Prospectus or Trust Agreement.

2) Exercise full investment discretion with regards to buying, managing, and selling assets held in the portfolios.

3) If managing a separate account (as opposed to a mutual fund or a commingled account), seek approval from the Client prior to purchasing and/or implementing the following securities and transactions:

—Letter stock and other unregistered securities; commodities or other commodity contracts; and short sales or margin transactions.

—Securities lending; pledging or hypothecating securities.

—Investments in the equity securities of any company with a record of less than three years continuous operation, including the operation of any predecessor.

—Investments for the purpose of exercising control of management.

4) Vote promptly all proxies and related actions in a manner consistent with the long-term interest and objectives of the Portfolio as described in this IPS. Each investment manager shall keep detailed records of the voting of proxies and related actions and will comply with all applicable regulatory obligations.

5) Communicate to the Client all significant changes pertaining to the fund it manages or the firm itself. Changes in ownership, organizational structure, financial condition, and professional staff are examples of changes to the firm in which the Client is interested.

6) Effect all transactions for the Portfolio subject "to best price and execution." If a manager utilizes brokerage from the Portfolio assets to effect "soft dollar" transactions, detailed records will be kept and communicated to the Client.

7) Use the same care, skill, prudence, and due diligence under the circumstances then prevailing that experienced investment professionals acting in a like capacity and fully familiar with such matters would use in like activities for like Portfolios with like aims in accordance and compliance with the Uniform Prudent Investor Act and all applicable laws, rules, and regulations.

8) If managing a separate account (as opposed to a mutual fund or a commingled account), acknowledge co-fiduciary responsibility by signing and returning a copy of this IPS.

Custodian

Custodians are responsible for the safekeeping of the Portfolio's assets. The specific duties and responsibilities of the custodian are:

1) Maintain separate accounts by legal registration.

2) Value the holdings.

3) Collect all income and dividends owed to the Portfolio.

4) Settle all transactions (buy-sell orders) initiated by the Investment Manager.

5) Provide monthly reports that detail transactions, cash flows, securities held and their current value, and change in value of each security and the overall portfolio since the previous report.

INVESTMENT MANAGER SELECTION

The Advisor will apply the following due diligence criteria in selecting each money manager or mutual fund.

1) Regulatory oversight: Each investment manager should be a regulated bank, an insurance company, a mutual fund organization, or a registered investment adviser.

2) Correlation to style or peer group: The product should be highly correlated to the asset class of the investment option. This is one of the most critical parts of the analysis since most of the remaining due diligence involves comparisons of the manager to the appropriate peer group.

3) Performance relative to a peer group: The product's performance should be evaluated against the peer group's median manager return, for 1-, 3- and 5-year cumulative periods.

4) Performance relative to assumed risk: The product's risk-adjusted performance (Alpha and/or Sharpe Ratio) should be evaluated against the peer group's median manager's risk-adjusted performance.

5) Minimum track record: The product's inception date should be greater than three years.

6) Assets under management: The product should have at least $75 million under management.

7) Holdings consistent with style: The screened product should have no more than 20% of the portfolio invested in "unrelated" asset class securities. For example, a Large-Cap Growth product should not hold more than 20% in cash, fixed income and/or international securities.

8) Expense ratios/fees: The product's fees should not be in the bottom quartile (most expensive) of their peer group.

9) Stability of the organization: There should be no perceived organizational problems—the same portfolio management team should be in place for at least two years.

CONTROL PROCEDURES

Performance Objectives

The Client acknowledges fluctuating rates of return characterize the securities markets, particularly during short-term time periods. Recognizing that short-term fluctuations may cause variations in performance, the Advisors intends to evaluate manager performance from a long-term perspective.

The Client is aware the ongoing review and analysis of the investment managers is just as important as the due diligence implemented during the manager selection process. The performance of the investment managers will be monitored on an ongoing basis and it is at the Client's discretion to take corrective action by replacing a manager if they deem it appropriate at any time.

On a timely basis, but not less than quarterly, the Advisor will meet with the Client to review whether each manager continues to conform to the search criteria outlined in the previous section; specifically:

1) The manager's adherence to the Portfolio's investment guidelines;
2) Material changes in the manager's organization, investment philosophy and/or personnel; and,
3) Any legal, SEC and/or other regulatory agency proceedings affecting the manager.

The Advisor has determined it is in the best interest of the Client that performance objectives be established for each investment manager. Manager performance will be evaluated in terms of an appropriate market index (e.g. the S&P 500 stock index for large-cap domestic equity manager) and the relevant peer group (e.g. the large-cap growth mutual fund universe for a large-cap growth mutual fund).

ASSET CLASS	INDEX	PEER GROUP
Large-Cap Equity		
Blend	S&P 500	Large-Cap Blend
Growth	Russell 200 Growth	Large-Cap Growth
Value	Russell 200 Value	Large-Cap Value
Mid-Cap Equity	S&P 400	Mid-Cap Blend
Small-Cap Equity	Russell 2000	Small-Cap Blend
International Equity	MSCI EAFE	Foreign Stock
Fixed Income		
Intermediate-Term Bond	Lehman Brothers Gov't/Credit Intermediate	Intermediate-Term Bond
Money Market	90-day T-Bills	Money Market Database

A manager may be placed on a *Watchlist* and a thorough *review* and *analysis* of the investment manager may be conducted, when:

1) A manager performs below median for their peer group over a 1-, 3- and/or 5-year cumulative period.
2) A manager's 3-year risk adjusted return (Alpha and/or Sharpe) falls below the peer group's median risk adjusted return.
3) There is a change in the professionals managing the portfolio.
4) There is a significant decrease in the product's assets.
5) There is an indication the manager is deviating from his/her stated style and/or strategy.

6) There is an increase in the product's fees and expenses.
7) Any extraordinary event occurs that may interfere with the manager's ability to fulfill their role in the future.

A manager evaluation may include the following steps:
1) A letter to the manager asking for an analysis of their underperformance.
2) An analysis of recent transactions, holdings and portfolio characteristics to determine the cause for underperformance or to check for a change in style.
3) A meeting with the manager, which may be conducted on-site, to gain insight into organizational changes and any changes in strategy or discipline.

The decision to retain or terminate a manager cannot be made by a formula. It is the Client's confidence in the manager's ability to perform in the future that ultimately determines the retention of a manager.

Measuring Costs

The Advisor will review with the Client at least annually all costs associated with the management of the Portfolio's investment program, including:
1) Expense ratios of each investment option against the appropriate peer group.
2) Custody fees: The holding of the assets, collection of the income and disbursement of payments.
3) Whether the manager is demonstrating attention to "best execution" in trading securities.

INVESTMENT POLICY REVIEW

The Advisor will review this IPS with the Client at least annually to determine whether stated investment objectives are still relevant and the continued feasibility of achieving the same. It is not expected that the IPS will change frequently. In particular, short-term changes in the financial markets should not require adjustments to the IPS.

Prepared:	Approved:
____________________	____________________
Advisor	Client
July 1, 2003	July 1, 2003

INVESTMENT POLICY STATEMENT
ABC Company (Defined Contribution Plan)

Approved on July 1, 2003
By ABC Company Investment Committee

This investment policy statement should be reviewed and updated at least annually. Any change to this policy should be communicated in writing on a timely basis to all interested parties.

This Investment Policy Statement (IPS) has been prepared by Fiduciary Analytics. It is intended to serve as an example of the type of information that would be included in a comprehensive IPS. Clients are advised to have legal counsel review their IPS before it is approved.

EXECUTIVE SUMMARY

Type of Plan:	Defined Contribution Plan—401(k)
Plan Sponsor:	ABC Company
Plan IRS Tax Identification:	56-1234567
Current Assets:	$20,000,000
Participant-Directed Investment Options:	Yes, 404(c) adopted
Frequency to Change Investment Options:	Daily
Investment Options:	Money Market (MM) Intermediate Bond (IB) Large-Cap Value (LCV) Large-Cap Blend (LCB) Large-Cap Growth (LCG) Mid-Cap Blend (MCB) Small-Cap Blend (SCB) International Equity (IE)

Evaluation Benchmarks and Modeled Portfolios:
Trustee Counseling Index™ (% Equity Exposure)*

	LCB	LCG	LCV	MCB	SCB	IE	IB	SB	MM
TCI (20)	5	5	5	0	0	5	40	30	10
TCI (40)	10	10	10	0	5	5	35	20	5
TCI (60)	10	10	10	10	10	10	35	0	5
TCI (80)	15	15	15	10	10	15	15	0	5

*The TCI™ series of indexes have several unique design features, two of which are:
1) They illustrate a series of prudently diversified portfolios; and
2) They illustrate the performance of a diversified portfolio, calculated using the performance of the median mutual fund manager for each peer group represented in the allocation.

PURPOSE

The purpose of this Investment Policy Statement (IPS) is to assist the ABC Company Employee Retirement Savings Plan Committee (Committee) [See Annex C] in effectively supervising, monitoring and evaluating the investment of the Company's Retirement Plan (Plan) assets. The Committee has the authority to oversee the investment of the Plan's assets. The Committee will discharge its responsibilities under the Plan solely in the interests of Plan participants and their beneficiaries. The Plan's investment program is defined in the various sections of this IPS by:

1) Stating in a written document the Committee's attitudes, expectations, objectives and guidelines for the investment of all Plan assets.

2) Encouraging effective communications between the Committee and service vendors by stating the responsibilities of the Committee, the investment managers, the investment consultant, and the record keepers and administrators.

3) Establishing the number and characteristics of offered investment options.

4) Providing rate-of-return and risk characteristics for each asset class represented by various investment options. [See Annex A]

5) Establishing procedures for selecting, monitoring, evaluating, and, if appropriate, replacing investment options.

6) Complying with all ERISA, fiduciary, prudence and due diligence requirements experienced investment professionals would utilize, and with all applicable laws, rules and regulations from various local, state, federal and international political entities that may impact the Plan assets.

This IPS has been formulated, based upon consideration by the Committee of the financial implications of a wide range of policies, and describes the prudent investment process the Committee deems appropriate.

BACKGROUND

The Plan is a defined contribution plan started in 1985 and is one of two qualified employee retirement plans sponsored by ABC Company. The purpose of the Plan is to encourage employees to build long-term careers with ABC Industries by providing eligible employees with a convenient way to save on a regular and long-term basis for retirement.

The Plan currently covers 2,500 employees. The number of employees is anticipated to increase at the rate of 5% per year for the next five years. Plan size is currently $20,000,000, and annual contributions should total $2,500,000 - $3,000,000.

Employee contributions are made through payroll deductions each payroll period and remitted to the trustee for investment into the employee designated investment options. The Company has elected to adopt 404(c) provisions, and provides a match of $1.00 for each $2.00 contributed by the participant.

Key Information

Name of Plan:	ABC Retirement Plan
Plan Sponsor:	ABC Company
Plan IRS Tax ID:	56-1234567
Related Retirement Plans:	ABC Defined Benefit Plan

Additional key information, which is subject to change from time-to-time, is contained in Annex ___ (the appropriate annex).

STATEMENT OF OBJECTIVES

This IPS has been arrived at upon consideration by the Committee by a wide range of policies, and describes the prudent investment process the Committee deems appropriate. This process includes offering various asset classes and investment management styles that, in total, are expected to offer participants a sufficient level of overall diversification and total investment return over the long-term. The objectives are:

1) Comply with Department of Labor 404(c) safe harbor provisions by:

a. Notifying participants that a 404(c) plan is constituted, including a statement that fiduciaries of the plan may be relieved of certain liabilities.
b. Providing participants at least three investment options that each have a different risk/return profile;
c. Providing participants with sufficient information so the participant can make an informed decision about his or her selection of investment option(s); and
d. Permitting participants to change investment options on a daily [quarterly] basis. Because each plan participant shall make investment contribution and allocation decisions, the Committee shall refrain from giving what could be construed as investment advice.

2) Have the ability to pay all benefit and expense obligations when due.

3) Control and account for all costs of administering the plan and managing the investments.

ASSET CLASS GUIDELINES

The Committee believes long-term investment performance, in large part, is primarily a function of asset class mix. The Committee has reviewed the long-term performance characteristics of the broad asset classes, focusing on balancing the risks and rewards.

History shows that while interest-generating investments, such as bond portfolios, have the advantage of relative stability of principal value, they provide little opportunity for real long-term capital growth due to their susceptibility to inflation. On the other hand, equity investments, such as common stocks, clearly have a significantly higher expected return but have the disadvantage of much greater year-by-year variability of return. From an investment decision-making point of view, this year-by-year variability may be worth accepting, provided the time horizon for the equity portion of the portfolio is sufficiently long (five years or greater).

The performance expectations (both risk and return) of each asset class are contained in Annex A. The following nine asset classes were selected and ranked in ascending order of "risk" (least to most): Money Market (MM), Short Bond (SB), Intermediate Bond (IB), Large Cap Value (LCV), Large Cap Blend (LCB), Large Cap Growth (LCG), Mid Cap Blend (MCB), Small Cap Blend (SCB), International Equity (IE).

The Committee has considered the following asset classes for inclusion in the asset mix, but has decided to exclude these asset classes at the present time: Global Fixed Income, Real Estate.

DUTIES AND RESPONSIBILITIES

Retirement Plan Committee

As fiduciaries under the Plan, the primary responsibilities of the Committee are:

1) Prepare and maintain this investment policy statement.
2) Provide sufficient asset classes with different and distinct risk/return profiles so each participant can prudently diversify his/her account.
3) Prudently select investment options.
4) Control and account for all investment, record keeping and administrative expenses associated with the Plan.
5) Monitor and supervise all service vendors and investment options.
6) Avoid prohibited transactions and conflicts of interest.

Investment Consultant

The Committee will retain an objective, third-party Consultant to assist the Committee in managing the overall investment process. The Consultant will be responsible for guiding the Committee through a disciplined and rigorous investment process to enable the Committee to meet the fiduciary responsibilities outlined above.

Investment Managers

As distinguished from the Committee and Consultant, who are responsible for *managing* the investment process, investment managers are responsible for *making* investment decisions (security selection and price decisions). The specific duties and responsibilities of each investment manager are:

1) Manage the assets under their supervision in accordance with the guidelines and objectives outlined in their respective Service Agreements, Prospectus or Trust Agreement.

2) Exercise full investment discretion with regards to buying, managing, and selling assets held in the portfolios.

3) Vote promptly all proxies and related actions in a manner consistent with the long-term interest and objectives of the Plan as described in this IPS. Each investment manager shall keep detailed records of the voting of proxies and related actions and will comply with all applicable regulatory obligations.

4) Communicate to the Committee all significant changes pertaining to the fund it manages or the firm itself. Changes in ownership, organizational structure, financial condition, and professional staff are examples of changes to the firm in which the Committee is interested.

5) Use the same care, skill, prudence, and due diligence under the circumstances then prevailing that experienced investment professionals acting in a like capacity and fully familiar with such matters would use in like activities for like retirement Plans with like aims in accordance and compliance with ERISA and all applicable laws, rules, and regulations.

Custodian

Custodians are responsible for the safekeeping of the Plan's assets. The specific duties and responsibilities of the custodian are:

1) Maintain separate accounts by legal registration.
2) Value the holdings.
3) Collect all income and dividends owed to the Plan.
4) Settle all transactions (buy-sell orders).
5) Provide monthly reports that detail transactions, cash flows, securities held and their current value, and change in value of each security and the overall portfolio since the previous report.

INVESTMENT MANAGER SELECTION

The Committee will apply the following due diligence criteria in selecting each money manager or mutual fund.

1) Regulatory oversight: Each investment manager should be a regulated bank, an insurance company, a mutual fund organization, or a registered investment adviser.

2) Correlation to style or peer group: The product should be highly correlated to the asset class of the investment option. This is one of the most critical parts of the analysis since most of the remaining due diligence involves comparisons of the manager to the appropriate peer group.

3) Performance relative to a peer group: The product's performance should be evaluated against the peer group's median manager return, for 1-, 3- and 5-year cumulative periods.

4) Performance relative to assumed risk: The product's risk-adjusted performance (Alpha and/or Sharpe Ratio) should be evaluated against the peer group's median manager's risk-adjusted performance.

5) Minimum track record: The product's inception date should be greater than three years.

6) Assets under management: The product should have at least $75 million under management.

7) Holdings consistent with style: The screened product should have no more than 20% of the portfolio invested in "unrelated" asset class securities. For example, a Large-Cap Growth product should not hold more than 20% in cash, fixed income and/or international securities.

8) Expense ratios/fees: The product's fees should not be in the bottom quartile (most expensive) of their peer group.

9) Stability of the organization: There should be no perceived organizational problems—the same portfolio management team should be in place for at least two years.

CONTROL PROCEDURES

Performance Objectives

The Committee acknowledges fluctuating rates of return characterize the securities markets, particularly during short-term time periods. Recognizing that short-term fluctuations may cause variations in performance, the Committee intends to evaluate manager performance from a long-term perspective.

The Committee is aware the ongoing review and analysis of the investment managers is just as important as the due diligence implemented during the manager selection process. The performance of the investment managers will be monitored on an ongoing basis and it is at the Committee's discretion to take corrective action by replacing a manager if they deem it appropriate at any time.

On a timely basis, but not less than quarterly, the Committee will meet to review whether each manager continues to conform to the search criteria outlined in the previous section; specifically:

1) The manager's adherence to the Plan's investment guidelines;
2) Material changes in the manager's organization, investment philosophy and/or personnel; and,
3) Any legal, SEC and/or other regulatory agency proceedings affecting the manager.

The Committee has determined it is in the best interest of the Plan's participants that performance objectives be established for each investment manager. Manager performance will be evaluated in terms of an appropriate market index (e.g. the S&P 500 stock index for large-cap domestic equity manager) and the relevant peer group (e.g. the large-cap growth mutual fund universe for a large-cap growth mutual fund).

ASSET CLASS	INDEX	PEER GROUP
Large-Cap Equity		
Blend	S&P 500	Large-Cap Blend
Growth	Russell 200 Growth	Large-Cap Growth
Value	Russell 200 Value	Large-Cap Value
Mid-Cap Equity	S&P 400	Mid-Cap Blend
Small-Cap Equity	Russell 2000	Small-Cap Blend
International Equity	MSCI EAFE	Foreign Stock
Fixed Income		
Intermediate-Term Bond	Lehman Brothers Gov't/ Credit Intermediate	Intermediate-Term Bond
Money Market	90-day T-Bills	Money Market Database

A manager may be placed on a *Watchlist* and a thorough *review* and *analysis* of the investment manager may be conducted, when:

1) A manager performs below median for their peer group over a 1-, 3- and/or 5-year cumulative period.
2) A manager's 3-year risk adjusted return (Alpha and/or Sharpe) falls below the peer group's median risk adjusted return.
3) There is a change in the professionals managing the portfolio.
4) There is a significant decrease in the product's assets.
5) There is an indication the manager is deviating from his/her stated style and/or strategy.
6) There is an increase in the product's fees and expenses.
7) Any extraordinary event occurs that may interfere with the manager's ability to fulfill their role in the future.

A manager evaluation may include the following steps:

1) A letter to the manager asking for an analysis of their underperformance.
2) An analysis of recent transactions, holdings and portfolio characteristics to determine the cause for underperformance or to check for a change in style.
3) A meeting with the manager, which may be conducted on-site, to gain insight into organizational changes and any changes in strategy or discipline.

The decision to retain or terminate a manager cannot be made by a formula. It is the Committee's confidence in the manager's ability to perform in the future that ultimately determines the retention of a manager.

Measuring Costs

The Committee will review at least annually all costs associated with the management of the Plan's investment program, including:

1) Expense ratios of each investment option against the appropriate peer group.

2) Custody fees: The holding of the assets, collection of the income and disbursement of payments.

3) Whether the manager is demonstrating attention to "best execution" in trading securities.

4) Administrative Fees: Costs to administer the Plan, including record keeping, account settlement (participant balance with that of fund), and allocation of assets and earnings, and (when applicable) the proper use of 12b-1 fees to offset these fees.

INVESTMENT POLICY REVIEW

The Committee will review this IPS at least annually to determine whether stated investment objectives are still relevant and the continued feasibility of achieving the same. It is not expected that the IPS will change frequently. In particular, short-term changes in the financial markets should not require adjustments to the IPS.

Prepared:	Approved:
____________________	____________________
Committee	Consultant
July 1, 2003	July 1, 2003

Appendix II

Subsequent Performance of Mutual Funds: Past Winners' Uncertain Future

A COMMON METHOD of evaluating mutual funds is to study the past performance of prospective funds; this is referred to as "track record investing." Although it is prudent to include past performance in a selection process, there are many other factors to consider alongside performance. This is so because history has shown that funds that have performed well in the past do not necessarily continue their superior performance into the future. The following charts illustrate the inability of funds to maintain above average performance over long periods of time.

Subsequent Performance of Top 30 Mutual Funds Five-Year Period: January 1971–December 1975

	FIVE-YEAR PERIOD Jan 71–Dec 75			SUBSEQUENT PERFORMANCE Jan 76–Dec 02		
	Rank	*% Rank*	*Annualized Return*	*Rank*	*% Rank*	*Annualized Return*
Janus Fund	1	1%	10.93	31	12%	14.37
Putnam Voyager/A	2	1%	10.67	25	10%	14.60
Mutual Shares Fund/Z	3	2%	10.38	4	2%	16.89
Pioneer Value/A	4	2%	10.01	45	18%	13.83
AIM Charter/A	5	3%	9.36	40	16%	14.06
INVESCO Core Equity/Inv	6	4%	8.49	59	24%	13.14
Lindner Large Cap Gr/Iv	7	4%	8.24	102	41%	11.90
Instl Inv Capital Apprec	8	5%	7.53	144	58%	10.67
Pioneer/A	9	5%	7.08	81	33%	12.61
Van Kampen Emerging Gr/A	10	6%	6.95	9	4%	15.75
SM&R:Equity Income Fund/T	11	6%	6.77	113	45%	11.66
Fidelity Contrafund	12	7%	6.58	26	10%	14.57
Neuberger Guardian/Inv	13	8%	6.43	90	36%	12.34
Neuberger Guardian/Tr	14	8%	6.41	98	39%	12.07
Lord Abbett Affiliated/A	15	9%	6.39	65	26%	13.05
Principal Capital Val/A	16	9%	6.29	119	48%	11.60
Amer Cnt Growth/Inv	17	10%	6.21	5	2%	16.77
MSB Fund	18	11%	5.90	107	43%	11.79
Washington Mutual Inv/A	19	11%	5.82	30	12%	14.46
Philadelphia Fund	20	12%	5.80	127	51%	11.21
Wade Fund	21	12%	5.66	182	73%	8.70
Putnam Investors/A	22	13%	5.57	111	45%	11.70
SAFECO Div Income/Inv	23	13%	5.45	130	52%	11.18
Evergreen Omega/A	24	14%	5.33	80	32%	12.68
Fidelity Destiny Pln I/O	25	15%	5.21	16	6%	15.43
Amer Cnt Select/Inv	26	15%	5.14	14	6%	15.53
American Mutual/A	27	16%	5.13	43	17%	13.86
T Rowe Price Sm Cp Stk	28	16%	5.02	17	7%	15.22
ING Corp Leaders/A	29	17%	4.85	94	38%	12.27
Delaware Decatur Eqty/A	30	17%	4.80	90	36%	12.34
Top 30 Funds Average Return			**6.81**			**13.21**
All Funds Average Return			**1.31**			**9.00**
S&P 500			**3.21**			**12.54**
No. of Funds			172			249
No. of Top 30 Funds > S&P 500			30			17

Sources: Standard & Poor's (excludes international, balanced, and specialty funds)

Subsequent Performance of Top 30 Mutual Funds Five-Year Period: January 1976–December 1980

	FIVE-YEAR PERIOD Jan 76–Dec 80			SUBSEQUENT PERFORMANCE Jan 81–Dec 02		
	Rank	*% Rank*	*Annualized Return*	*Rank*	*% Rank*	*Annualized Return*
Amer Cnt Growth/Inv	1	0%	52.14	138	50%	9.95
Alliance Quasar/A	2	1%	41.56	184	67%	8.21
Evergreen/I	3	1%	40.92	162	59%	8.91
Security: Mid Cap Gr/A	4	2%	40.13	196	71%	7.53
Fidelity Magellan	5	2%	39.86	2	1%	15.74
Amer Cnt Select/Inv	6	2%	36.84	88	32%	11.17
Oppenheimer Gr/A	7	3%	36.27	174	63%	8.60
Value Line Lever Grth Inv	8	3%	35.90	73	27%	11.58
Value Line Spcl Situation	9	4%	35.74	186	68%	8.14
Liberty Acorn Fund/Z	10	4%	35.02	13	5%	13.87
AIM Constellation/A	11	4%	34.72	131	48%	10.08
AIM Weingarten/A	12	5%	34.42	139	51%	9.81
Van Kampen Pace/A	13	5%	33.73	111	40%	10.52
Lindner Large Cap Gr/Iv	14	6%	33.13	194	71%	7.56
T Rowe Price Sm Cp Stk	15	6%	32.76	74	27%	11.57
Dreyfus Growth Opport	16	6%	32.60	203	74%	6.69
Evergreen Emerging Gr/B	17	7%	32.56	201	73%	6.86
MFS Growth Opport/A	18	7%	31.89	154	56%	9.19
Hartford Growth Opp/L	19	8%	31.67	83	30%	11.32
Spectra Fund/N	20	8%	31.61	30	11%	12.98
Capstone Growth Fund	21	8%	31.37	161	59%	8.92
SAFECO Growth Opp/Inv	22	9%	31.24	137	50%	9.98
Pioneer Value/A	23	9%	31.08	124	45%	10.24
Value Line Fund	24	10%	30.88	155	56%	9.17
Scudder Development/S	25	10%	30.61	202	74%	6.79
AIM Charter/A	26	10%	30.59	106	39%	10.61
AXP Growth Fund/A	27	11%	30.52	119	43%	10.39
Vanguard Explorer	28	11%	30.28	153	56%	9.30
Van Kampen Emerging Gr/A	29	12%	30.05	36	13%	12.73
Scudder Dynamic Gr/A	30	12%	29.74	198	72%	7.11
Top 30 Funds Average Return			**34.33**			**9.85**
All Funds Average Return			**15.83**			**7.74**
S&P 500			**13.95**			**12.22**
No. of Funds			249			275
No. of Top 30 Funds > S&P 500			30			4

Sources: Standard & Poor's (excludes international, balanced, and specialty funds)

Subsequent Performance of Top 30 Mutual Funds Five-Year Period: January 1981–December 1985

	FIVE-YEAR PERIOD Jan 81–Dec 85			SUBSEQUENT PERFORMANCE Jan 86–Dec 02		
	Rank	*% Rank*	*Annualized Return*	*Rank*	*% Rank*	*Annualized Return*
Fidelity Magellan	1	0%	28.39	37	10%	12.26
OppenQst: Val/A	2	1%	27.72	155	40%	10.18
Sequoia Fund	3	1%	25.20	5	1%	14.82
Mosaic Eq Investors Fund	4	2%	23.77	157	40%	10.16
CGM Capital Development	5	2%	23.60	68	17%	11.42
Lindner Large Cap Gr/Iv	6	2%	23.58	327	84%	3.26
Vanguard Windsor/Inv	7	3%	23.10	99	25%	10.94
Fidelity Destiny Pln I/O	8	3%	22.36	128	33%	10.56
Mutual Qualified Fund/Z	9	3%	22.21	24	6%	12.77
Phoenix-Engemann: Cap Gr/A	10	4%	22.11	293	75%	7.27
Evergreen Eqty Inc/I	11	4%	21.83	274	70%	7.78
Salomon Bros: Opportunity	12	4%	21.54	158	40%	10.15
Phoenix-Engemann: Agg Gr/A	13	5%	21.51	242	62%	8.50
Fidelity Equity Income	14	5%	21.35	122	31%	10.60
Washington Mutual Inv/A	15	6%	21.25	27	7%	12.69
Nicholas Fund	16	6%	21.11	209	54%	9.21
CDC Nvest Targeted Eq/A	17	6%	20.93	177	45%	9.94
Ivy: Growth Fund/A	18	7%	20.71	316	81%	5.63
Guardian Park Avenue/A	19	7%	20.62	121	31%	10.61
Van Kampen Pace/A	20	7%	20.49	276	71%	7.75
W&R Advisors Core Inv/A	21	8%	20.40	60	15%	11.64
Principal Capital Val/A	22	8%	20.08	250	64%	8.35
ING Magna Cap/A	23	8%	19.97	216	55%	9.05
WPG Tudor	24	9%	19.85	284	73%	7.55
Royce: PA Mutual/Inv	25	9%	19.76	106	27%	10.85
Federated Amer Ldrs/A	26	10%	19.75	173	44%	9.99
Gartmore Growth/D	27	10%	19.74	317	81%	5.62
Salomon Bros: Capital/O	28	10%	19.65	73	19%	11.32
Mutual Shares Fund/Z	29	11%	19.49	25	6%	12.74
SAFECO Div Income/Inv	30	11%	19.41	283	72%	7.56
Top 30 Funds Average Return			**21.72**			**9.71**
All Funds Average Return			**10.93**			**7.99**
S&P 500			**14.72**			**11.50**
No. of Funds			275			391
No. of Top 30 Funds > S&P 500			30			6

Sources: Standard & Poor's (excludes international, balanced, and specialty funds)

Subsequent Performance of Top 30 Mutual Funds Five-Year Period: January 1986–December 1990

	FIVE-YEAR PERIOD Jan 86–Dec 90			SUBSEQUENT PERFORMANCE Jan 91–Dec 02		
	Rank	*% Rank*	*Annualized Return*	*Rank*	*% Rank*	*Annualized Return*
Fidelity Destiny Pln II/O	1	0%	21.03	43	7%	13.89
AIM Weingarten/A	2	1%	17.00	534	85%	5.52
Strong Opportunity/Inv	3	1%	16.96	98	16%	12.50
Fidelity Grth & Inc	4	1%	16.21	87	14%	12.74
Janus Venture	5	1%	15.92	358	57%	9.27
Nicholas-App US Eqty Gr/I	6	2%	15.91	406	65%	8.75
AXP New Dimensions/A	7	2%	15.58	148	24%	11.68
Fidelity Congress Street	8	2%	15.42	225	36%	10.76
Fidelity Adv Eq Grth/Is	9	2%	15.30	93	15%	12.65
AIM Charter/A	10	3%	14.97	394	63%	8.82
Fidelity Contrafund	11	3%	14.89	29	5%	14.97
PIMCO: PEA Grth/C	12	3%	14.86	484	77%	7.37
Amer Cnt Ultra/Inv	13	3%	14.83	84	13%	12.88
Berger Growth Fund	14	4%	14.62	515	82%	6.40
Fidelity Magellan	15	4%	14.55	176	28%	11.33
Columbia Special/Z	16	4%	14.44	143	23%	11.75
Janus Fund	17	4%	14.43	340	54%	9.46
Putnam Voyager/A	18	5%	14.25	187	30%	11.23
SmBarney Aggr Growth/A	19	5%	14.03	34	5%	14.80
Amer Cnt Giftrust/Inv	19	5%	14.03	266	42%	10.31
Quant Growth & Inc/Ord	21	5%	13.95	327	52%	9.59
Delaware Core Equity/A	22	6%	13.91	429	68%	8.43
Phoenix-Engemann: Cap Gr/A	23	6%	13.90	547	87%	4.62
FPA Paramount	24	6%	13.89	544	87%	4.73
Davis New York Venture/A	25	6%	13.78	51	8%	13.65
Fidelity Exchange	26	7%	13.73	257	41%	10.38
Federated Grth Strat/A	27	7%	13.72	403	64%	8.77
Amer Cnt Growth/Inv	28	7%	13.71	388	62%	8.89
AXP Stock Fund/A	29	7%	13.69	461	73%	7.96
ING Corp Leaders/A	30	8%	13.68	287	46%	10.15
Top 30 Funds Average Return			**14.91**			**10.14**
All Funds Average Return			**8.01**			**8.89**
S&P 500			**13.14**			**10.82**
No. of Funds			391			628
No. of Top 30 Funds > S&P 500			30			12

Sources: Standard & Poor's (excludes international, balanced, and specialty funds)

Subsequent Performance of Top 30 Mutual Funds Five-Year Period: January 1991–December 1995

	FIVE-YEAR PERIOD Jan 91–Dec 95			SUBSEQUENT PERFORMANCE Jan 96–Dec 02		
	Rank	*% Rank*	*Annualized Return*	*Rank*	*% Rank*	*Annualized Return*
Amer Cnt Giftrust/Inv	1	0%	35.10	1655	96%	–4.56
PBHG Growth	2	0%	35.08	1655	96%	–4.56
AIM Aggressive Growth/A	3	1%	34.21	1356	78%	2.04
Putnam New Opport/A	4	1%	33.37	1480	86%	0.38
PIMCO: PEA Opportunity/A	5	1%	32.64	1570	91%	–1.27
PIMCO: PEA Opportunity/C	6	1%	31.71	1593	92%	–2.00
Oppenheimer Main St G&I/A	7	1%	30.62	861	50%	5.24
MFS Emerg Growth/B	8	1%	30.51	1592	92%	–1.86
FPA Capital	9	1%	28.96	42	2%	13.15
Federated Kaufmann/K	10	2%	28.63	449	26%	7.16
Delaware Trend/A	11	2%	27.38	442	26%	7.21
Putnam OTC Emerg Gr/A	12	2%	27.29	1708	99%	–9.11
Heartland Grp: Value Fund	13	2%	27.25	167	10%	9.84
SunAmerica Eq New Cent/A	14	2%	27.21	1473	85%	0.46
State St Rsch: Md Cp Gr/S	15	2%	26.94	1606	93%	–2.25
Montgomery Sm Cap/R	16	3%	26.93	1526	88%	–0.40
CGM Capital Development	17	3%	26.78	1429	83%	1.14
Evergreen Emerging Gr/B	18	3%	26.58	1591	92%	–1.82
W&R Advisors New Cncpts/A	19	3%	26.57	1009	58%	4.43
Oberweis: Emerging Growth	20	3%	26.27	1378	80%	1.76
T Rowe Price New Horizons	21	3%	26.22	1174	68%	3.43
Seligman Frontier/A	22	4%	26.20	1619	94%	–2.64
RSI Retire Emerg Growth	23	4%	26.04	1543	89%	–0.66
AIM Constellation/A	24	4%	25.83	1346	78%	2.16
Spectra Fund/N	25	4%	25.77	1012	59%	4.41
Strong Adv Common Stock/Z	26	4%	25.63	299	17%	8.35
Pioneer Mid Cap Value/A	27	4%	25.37	616	36%	6.34
Amer Cnt Ultra/Inv	28	5%	25.01	917	53%	4.95
INVESCO Dynamics/Inv	29	5%	24.88	1187	69%	3.34
M Stanley Inst: Sm Vl/Is	30	5%	24.68	269	16%	8.72
Top 30 Funds Average Return			**28.19**			**2.11**
All Funds Average Return			**15.70**			**4.68**
S&P 500			**16.57**			**6.89**
No. of Funds			627			1729
No. of Top 30 Funds > S&P 500			30			6

Sources: Standard & Poor's (excludes international, balanced, and specialty funds)

Subsequent Performance of Top 30 Mutual Funds Five-Year Period: January 1996–December 2000

	FIVE-YEAR PERIOD Jan 96–Dec 00			SUBSEQUENT PERFORMANCE Jan 01–Dec 02		
	Rank	*% Rank*	*Annualized Return*	*Rank*	*% Rank*	*Annualized Return*
Goldman Sachs CORE LCG/A	1	0%	55.02	3536	77%	−24.28
Calamos Growth/A	2	0%	37.24	1230	27%	−11.88
Bridgeway: Aggr Inv/1	3	0%	36.01	1699	37%	−14.67
First Amer MicroCap/Y	4	0%	35.81	1175	26%	−11.44
First Amer MicroCap/A	5	0%	35.43	1202	26%	−11.67
Rydex: OTC/Inv	6	0%	32.34	4492	97%	−36.63
Van Kampen Growth/A	7	0%	31.44	3267	71%	−22.42
RS: Emerging Growth/A	8	1%	31.33	4410	96%	−34.04
Fidelity New Millennium	9	1%	30.91	2687	58%	−19.02
Van Kampen Growth/B	10	1%	30.60	3365	73%	−22.98
Van Kampen Growth/C	11	1%	30.59	3359	73%	−22.95
Janus Olympus	11	1%	30.59	4184	91%	−30.15
Meridian Value Fund	13	1%	29.36	352	8%	−1.62
State St Rsch: Aurora/S	14	1%	29.34	443	10%	−3.27
Delaware Select Grth/A	15	1%	29.12	4082	89%	−28.88
SmBarney Aggr Growth/Z	16	1%	28.99	2813	61%	−19.61
White Oak Growth	17	1%	28.97	4537	98%	−39.53
State St Rsch: Aurora/A	18	1%	28.93	460	10%	−3.61
IPS Millennium Fund	19	1%	28.91	4451	97%	−35.36
Van Kampen Emerging Gr/A	20	1%	28.33	4372	95%	−32.91
SmBarney Aggr Growth/A	20	1%	28.33	2869	62%	−19.92
Phoenix-Engemann: Sm Mid/A	22	1%	28.25	4192	91%	−30.25
Legg Mason Eq: Value/I	23	1%	28.15	1453	32%	−13.36
Delaware Select Grth/C	23	1%	28.15	4128	90%	−29.41
Heritage Srs Grth Eqty/A	25	1%	27.99	3310	72%	−22.7
State St Rsch: Aurora/C	26	2%	27.95	506	11%	−4.3
State St Rsch: Aurora/B	26	2%	27.95	480	10%	−3.85
Touchstone Growth Opp/A	28	2%	27.77	4332	94%	−32.21
ING Small Cap Opp/A	29	2%	27.67	4542	99%	−39.79
Van Wagoner Emerging Grth	30	2%	27.66	4610	100%	−62.21
Top 30 Funds Average Return			**30.97**			**−22.83**
All Funds Average Return			**15.23**			**−17.21**
S&P 500			**18.35**			**−17.15**
No. of Funds			1729			4611
No. of Top 30 Funds > S&P 500			30			10

Sources: Standard & Poor's (excludes international, balanced, and specialty funds)

NOTES

Introduction

1. Ric Edelman, *Inside Personal Finance* (January 1999; updated September 26, 2003).

2. A detailed account of the tulip bulb craze can be found in *Extraordinary Popular Delusions and the Madness of Crowds,* by Charles Mackey. First Templeton Foundation Press paperback edition November 1999, p. 89–97.

3. While this study has its critics, I can say from my own experience as an adviser for more than sixteen years that I have seen many real-world examples that support its findings.

4. "Your Own Worst Enemy," by Mathew Miller, *Forbes,* Dec. 22, 2003.

5. There is no legislation governing fiduciary responsibility for individual and family accounts when assets are not held in trust. However, the language of the UPIA would most likely govern these types of accounts.

PART ONE: MODERN PORTFOLIO THEORY
Chapter One: Early Years

1. Peter L. Bernstein, *Capital Ideas* (New York: The Free Press, 1992), p. 33.

2. *Capital Ideas,* pp. 35–36.

3. One measure of the importance of the Cowles Commission is that nearly every recipient of the Nobel Prize in Economics has been associated in some way with the Commission.

4. Fiduciaries do not have to be mathematical geniuses, but they are required under standards of prudent fiduciary investing to have a basic understanding of the principles of Modern Portfolio Theory. While the Restatement notes that "[t]here are no universally accepted and enduring theories of financial markets or prescriptions for investment that can provide clear and specific guidance to trustees and courts," the prefatory note to the Uniform Prudent Investor Act and the Introduction to the Restatement nonetheless emphasize the pervasive influence of Modern Portfolio Theory on prudent fiduciary investing. In fact, the primary reason for drafting the Restatement (and the Act subsequently) was to recognize and accept many of the tenets of Modern Portfolio Theory.

5. This emphasis on the *portfolio* (instead of individual stocks) as the unit that investors should be concerned with is why the body of scholarly work that Markowitz started (and which others have added to over the years) is known as Modern *Portfolio* Theory.

6. *Capital Ideas,* pp. 57 and 64.

7. Roger G. Ibbotson and Rex A. Sinquefield, "Stocks, Bonds, Bills and Inflation: Year-by-Year Historical Returns (1926–1974)," *Journal of Business,* 49:1 (January 1976), pp. 11–47.

8. Dimensional Fund Advisors Returns Program: This is an excellent tool for analyzing market and investment data. It is available to approved individuals only; please visit their website for more information: www.dfaus.com.

9. Paul H. Cootner, ed., *The Random Character of Stock Prices* (Cambridge, MA: The MIT Press, 1964).

10. See *Theorie de la Speculation* by Louis Bachelier (Paris: Gauthier-Villars, 1900).

11. Paul A. Samuelson, "Proof That Properly Anticipated Prices Fluctuate Randomly," *Industrial Management Review,* Spring 1965, pp. 42.

12. Eugene F. Fama, "Random Walks in Stock Market Prices," *Financial Analysts Journal,* September/October 1965, pp. 55–59.

13. Restatement Third of Trusts (Prudent Investor Rule), 1992, p. 75.

Chapter Two: Practical Applications

1. The CAPM posits that there is only one determinant of stock returns, and that is the stock market itself. As a result, the CAPM is said to be a "one-factor" model.

2. A serious criticism of the CAPM is that past betas of stocks do not necessarily extend into the future.

3. A stock with a beta of 0.8 has an expected return that is 20 percent less than the stock market, and is 20 percent less risky than the market. Stocks with betas less than 1.0 are less volatile and thus have *lower* expected returns than the market portfolio.

4. Sharpe assumed that the market portfolio included all the risky assets in the world, but for practical purposes we will assume that market portfolio is a total market index, such as the Wilshire 5000.

5. Fiduciaries should be aware that there are other proxies for the risk-free rate of return as well.

6. The 3-year average Treasury bill rate is used to make the calculations easier to understand.

7. Eugene Fama Jr., "Multi Factor Investing," January 1996, p. 3 of 26-page internally written white paper, Dimensional Fund Advisors.

8. Fama and French do not anticipate the market risk factor to deliver

this type of premium over Treasury bills in the future. Their current, much more conservative estimate is about 3.3 percent.

9. The definitions of small, large, value, growth, and the calculated risk premiums of the three risk factors are complex and beyond the scope of this book. For a complete and current description, please see the website of Kenneth French at http://mba.tuck.Dartmouth.edu/pages/faculty/ken.French/data_library.html. In addition, an excellent discussion on the size and value effects, including value and growth construction methodologies, can be found in the 2003 edition of *Stocks, Bonds, Bills and Inflation,* pp. 123–169.

10. For example, an earnings-to-asset ratio of 4.21 means a company generates $4.21 for every $100 of company assets.

11. Michelle Clayman, "In Search of Excellence: The Investors Viewpoint," *Financial Analysts Journal* (May–June 1987), p. 63.

Part Two: The 5 Steps and Twenty-Seven Practices

Step One: Analyze Current Position

1. There is no legislation governing fiduciary responsibility for individual and family accounts when assets are not held in trust. However, the language of the UPIA would most likely govern these types of accounts.

2. Some doctors and other professionals that feel vulnerable to potential lawsuits as a result of professional conduct have established offshore trust accounts in order to protect their personal assets.

Step Two: Diversity—Allocate Portfolio

1. This TRR calculation is simplified. To accurately determine the TRR you need to know what terminal account value the investor wishes to have at death. If the investor is an individual, the options are inflation-adjusted original principal, nominal principal, willing to spend principal, etc. The TRR calculations for defined benefit plans, foundations and endowments is beyond the scope of this book.

Step Three: Formalize Investment Policy

1. See "Why a Brokerage Giant Pushes Some Mediocre Mutual Funds," *The Wall Street Journal,* January 1, 2004.

Step Four: Implement Policy

1. Reporter's General Note on Restatement Section 227, Comments *e* through *h*, p. 79.

Step Five: Monitor and Supervise

1. U.S. Department of Labor, "Study of 401(k) Plan Fees and Expenses," issued April 13, 1998.

Continuing-Education Exam

for CFP Continuing-Education Credit
and PACE Recertification Credit

EARN TEN HOURS of credit toward your CFP Board CE requirement as well as PACE Recertification credit by passing the following exam online at **www.bloomberg.com/ce**, and entering code **FS88HN38.**

All the material has been previewed by the CFP Board of Standards. If you wish to find out if this book and exam can be used to fulfill the CE requirement for a different organization, please contact its governing board directly.

INTRODUCTION

1. Which of the following does not describe a fiduciary?

a. someone that has a legal or moral responsibility for managing property for the benefit of another
b. a stockbroker rendering an opinion on a particular stock
c. someone exercising control, authority, or discretion over assets
d. someone acting in a professional capacity rendering advice on a continuous basis

2. What type of accounts are governed by the Employee Retirement Income Security Act (ERISA)?

a. private trusts
b. charitable trusts
c. retirement plans
d. foundations/endowments

3. Which of the following is not true regarding the Restatement 3rd of Trusts?

a. It was issued in 1992.

b. It states that risk and return are directly related.
c. Sound diversification is fundamental to risk management.
d. The primary focus of the portfolio is on the individual investments.

PART ONE: Modern Portfolio Theory

4. Prior to the 1950s, which statement best described the investment philosophy of the time?

a. Diversification is desirable.
b. Diversification is undesirable.

5. Which statement is true regarding Harry Markowitz's *Portfolio Selection*?

a. The central concern of investing is expected return.
b. Individual stocks lose much of their risk when properly combined together in a portfolio.
c. A portfolio is inefficient when it offers the highest return for a given level of risk.
d. The process of mean variance optimization utilizes beta.

6. Stand deviation is a measure of

a. risk
b. volatility
c. range of returns
d. all of the above

7. One standard deviation measures what percent of all possible outcomes?

a. 100%
b. 68%
c. 95%
d. 50%

8. The Center for Research in Security Prices (CRSP) determined that the return for stocks for the period 1926–1960 was approximately

a. 12%
b. 15%
c. 9%
d. 7.5%

9. The Ibbotson-Sinquefield data for the period 1926–2003 shows what asset class as having had the highest return?

a. T-bills
b. large stocks
c. small stocks
d. long-term government bonds

10. Which statement best describes the conclusion of the Random Walk Theory?

a. Past movements of stock prices can be used to predict future movements.
b. Regardless of a security's last price movement, the probability is equal that the next move will be up or down.
c. Past security price movements are correlated to future movements.
d. Technical analysis is a valid investment strategy.

11. The Efficient Market Theory states:

a. It is possible to identify underpriced securities.
b. In an efficient market, the current price of a security is a good estimate of its intrinsic value.
c. There can be a disproportionate number of investors profiting consistently above market returns.
d. all of the above

12. The Capital Asset Pricing Model is a:

a. two-factor model
b. three-factor model
c. one-factor model
d. four-factor model

13. In the Capital Asset Pricing Model total risk is measured by adding compensated and uncompensated risk.

a. true
b. false

14. According to the Capital Asset Pricing Model, which type of risk can be reduced or eliminated through diversification?

a. credit risk
b. inflation risk
c. compensated risk
d. uncompensated risk

15. Alpha is a measure of:

a. a portfolio's gross return
b. return above what is expected given a portfolio's beta
c. only positive returns
d. none of the above

16. Which of the following is not a factor within the Fama-French Three-Factor model?

a. market
b. size
c. interest
d. value

17. According to the Fama-French Three-Factor Model, increasing risk in a portfolio is done by increasing what type of stocks in the portfolio?

a. large growth
b. small growth
c. real estate investment trusts
d. small value

PART TWO: The Five Steps and Twenty-Seven Practices

18. Which of the following account types have no particular legislation or oversight body governing them?

a. individual and family
b. private trusts
c. foundations
d. corporate retirement plans

19. In an instance where the terms of a private trust are in conflict with the Uniform Prudent Investors Act (UPIA), the terms of the trust would prevail.

a. true
b. false

20. The primary duty of the fiduciary is to manage the overall investment process. Which of the following is among the seven fundamental responsibilities of a fiduciary?

a. prepare investment policy statement
b. control and account for investment expenses
c. avoid conflicts of interest and prohibited transactions
d. all of the above

21. With respect to a retirement plan which of the following are not a "party-in-interest"?

a. a person providing services to the plan
b. a fiduciary of the plan
c. a spouse of a fiduciary
d. a CPA providing services to a participant in the plan

22. Which of the following factors is not needed to estimate future stock returns?

a. initial dividend yield of the market
b. estimated growth in earnings
c. fed funds rate
d. estimate of expansion or contraction in P/E multiple

23. In the Hierarchy of Decisions, which is the least important consideration?

a. What asset classes will be considered?
b. What is the time horizon of the investment strategy?
c. Which managers/funds will be considered?
d. What will be the mix among asset classes?

24. Adding an asset class to a portfolio should be done to:

a. increase the risk of the portfolio
b. decrease the risk of the portfolio
c. maximize the tax efficiency of the portfolio
d. improve the risk/return ratio of the portfolio

25. Which of the following is not a priority of the Investment Policy Statement?

a. defining the responsibilities of all parties involved in the management of portfolio assets
b. defining the monitoring criteria for selected investment options
c. defining the economic indicators that may warrant changes to the investment policy
d. defining the control procedures for accounting of investment expenses

26. Primary benefit(s) of defining rebalancing guidelines is:

a. maintains the portfolio's desired risk level
b. forces a policy of "buy low, sell high"

c. both A and B
d. none of the above

27. Which statement(s) is true of active and passive investment strategies?

a. Both are prudent strategies.
b. The burden of proof for the validity of its value is greatest with the active strategy.
c. both A and B
d. none of the above

28. The ERISA safe harbor rules pertaining to decisions made by investment committees include:

a. Use prudent experts to make investment decisions.
b. Give the prudent expert non-discretion over the portfolio.
c. both A and B
d. none of the above

29. Which of the following is not required in order for a 401(k) plan sponsor to reduce liability under 404c?

a. Choose from a broad range of investment options, which consist of at least four diversified investment options.
b. Give investment instruction at least quarterly.
c. Obtain sufficient information to make informed decisions.
d. Diversify investments within and among investment alternatives.

30. Which of the following is not a benefit of mutual funds?

a. greater liquidity—ease in entering and exiting
b. easier in meeting asset allocation and rebalancing guidelines
c. eliminates phantom tax consequences
d. easier to conduct due-diligence

31. Periodic reports should be prepared to compare investment performance against all of the following except:

a. appropriate index
b. IPS objectives
c. client expectations
d. peer groups

32. Which is not true about soft dollars?

a. They are an illegal overcharge for a trade.
b. They are services provided out of excess profit earned on a trade.
c. Services received from soft dollars include research and technology.
d. Accounts affected must benefit directly or indirectly from services received from soft dollars.

33. Of the following fees, what cannot be paid directly from retirement plan assets?

a. fees for plan design
b. fees for selection and monitoring of investment options
c. fees for recordkeeping
d. fees for investment management

34. The Department of Labor has identified specific levels of fees that may be charged to retirement plans.

a. true
b. false

35. The original intent of 12b-1 fees was to:

a. compensate the fund manager
b. defray the cost of marketing and distribution of fund shares
c. compensate brokers for ongoing service
d. none of the above

INDEX

About Bloomberg

BLOOMBERG L.P., founded in 1981, is a global information services, news, and media company. Headquartered in New York, the company has sales and news operations worldwide.

Bloomberg, serving customers on six continents, holds a unique position within the financial services industry by providing an unparalleled range of features in a single package known as the BLOOMBERG PROFESSIONAL® service. By addressing the demand for investment performance and efficiency through an exceptional combination of information, analytic, electronic trading, and Straight Through Processing tools, Bloomberg has built a worldwide customer base of corporations, issuers, financial intermediaries, and institutional investors.

BLOOMBERG NEWS®, founded in 1990, provides stories and columns on business, general news, politics, and sports to leading newspapers and magazines throughout the world. BLOOMBERG TELEVISION®, a 24-hour business and financial news network, is produced and distributed globally in seven different languages. BLOOMBERG RADIO℠ is an international radio network anchored by flagship station BLOOMBERG® 1130 (WBBR-AM) in New York.

In addition to the BLOOMBERG PRESS® line of books, Bloomberg publishes *BLOOMBERG MARKETS®* and *BLOOMBERG WEALTH MANAGER®* magazines. To learn more about Bloomberg, call a sales representative at:

London:	+44-20-7330-7500
New York:	+1-212-318-2000
Tokyo:	+81-3-3201-8900

FOR IN-DEPTH MARKET INFORMATION and news, visit the Bloomberg website at **www.bloomberg.com**, which draws from the news and power of the BLOOMBERG PROFESSIONAL® service and Bloomberg's host of media products to provide high-quality news and information in multiple languages on stocks, bonds, currencies, and commodities.

About the Author

TIM HATTON, a Certified Financial Planner practitioner and Certified Investment Management Analyst, earned the designation of Accredited Investment Fiduciary at the Center for Fiduciary Studies, the nationally recognized training organization affiliated with the Foundation for Fiduciary Studies. He is founder and president of Hatton Consulting Inc., a registered investment adviser, in Phoenix, Arizona. His firm specializes in delivering to investors an investment process that adheres to a fiduciary standard of care. In addition to managing assets for investors, Mr. Hatton consults with CPAs, attorneys, retirement plan sponsors, trustees, and other financial advisers on the merits and benefits of a fiduciary standard of care. Before starting that firm, he served for thirteen years with Morgan Stanley, most recently as senior vice president of investments. He holds a B.S. in Business Administration from the University of Arizona.

About the Foundation for Fiduciary Studies

THE FOUNDATION FOR FIDUCIARY STUDIES (www.ffstudies.org) is a not-for-profit organization established to develop and advance the practices that define a prudent process for investment fiduciaries, who include trustees and investment committee members as well as brokers, bankers, and investment advisers. It is independent of ties to the investment community.

About the Center for Fiduciary Studies

THE FOUNDATION operates in association with the Center for Fiduciary Studies (www.cfstudies.com), which was established as the first full-time training and research facility focused exclusively on investment fiduciary responsibility and portfolio management. The Center provides training to help investment fiduciaries and professionals understand the intersection between their responsibilities and the investment process. At the Center, professionals can study and earn the Accredited Investment Fiduciary (AIF®) and Accredited Investment Fiduciary Auditor (AIFA®) professional designations.

The Center is headquartered at the University of Pittsburgh Joseph M. Katz Graduate School of Business's Center for Executive Education, with additional locations in Orlando and Seattle. The Center is registered as a sponsor of continuing professional education with the Certified Financial Planner™ (CFP®) Board of Standards, the Investment Management Consultants Association (IMCA), and the National Association of State Boards of Accountancy (NASBA) National Registry of CPE Sponsors.

About Fiduciary Analytics

FIDUCIARY ANALYTICS is the technology arm that develops web-based tools based on the Foundation's fiduciary practices for investment decision makers. Additional information and resources for fiduciaries can be found at the Fiduciary Analytics website, www.fi360.com.